T0328750

FLAME AND SONG

FLAME AND SONG

A MEMOIR

Philippa Namutebi Kabali-Kagwa

Flame and Song
Text © Philippa Namutebi Kabali-Kagwa

ISBN (Print): 9781928215219
ISBN (Digital download): 9781928215226

Lighting the Ashes

Today
I picked up
that instrument
that I had strung and unstrung
for so long,
threw it into the fire,
opened my mouth
and
sang.

My voice
rang out
loud and clear.

Becoming one with the fire.

The flames of my belly-heart
shaped the song
that danced out on my voice
rekindling the ashes.

Today I sang
the song I had come
to sing.

And my fire burns again.

Dedication

To my parents, Fayce and Henry Barlow, whose love, strength, courage, resilience and generosity shaped who I am in the world today. To my sister Fay and brother Chris, whose cerebral palsy was a blessing in disguise. Thank you for teaching me to listen with my heart, to see with my eyes and my body, for teaching me courage and wisdom, and for helping me understand from an early age that we are more than our bodies. To my sisters Maliza and Estella, who were there from the start.

To my husband Victor, who has travelled more than half my life with me, and who has lived in parts of this landscape, with his own story to tell.

To my children: Faye, who is my greatest supporter and critic, thank you for listening to my stories and for your inspiration and insight. Senteza, whose big heart and quick temper keep me grounded and on my toes. And Chris, who keeps me young. I hope this gives you some insight into the experiences that have shaped me.

To all Ugandans who have lived through the first 50 years of independence: those who have loved Uganda deeply, and are proud of being Ugandan, and those who, over the years, have felt anger, shame, fear and frustration at being called Ugandan. As a generation, we have a story to tell, about the impact of war, about starting over at home or in foreign lands, and about who and what has kept us alive and hoping.

The history books tell us about explorers, despotic leaders, economic war, HIV and foreign policy, but they omit the voices of the people who lived through it. We are the keepers of these stories; they are ours to tell.

It is my hope that my story will inspire others to tell theirs, too, so they will not be forgotten.

Contents

Prologue

We burn up with flames – of love, hope, fear, rage –
and then burn out. And always an ember still glows.

My father always called us 'Love'. There was something in the way he said it. *Love.* It was his special name for us. There were five of us children – Maliza, Estella, Fay, Chris and me. But his heart was big enough to love many, so many.

In a letter he wrote to me when I was at boarding school, he told me how he had looked outside that morning at the glistening grass and called Maama to show her the thousands of diamonds he would have bought her, had he had the money. My mother's response was, 'It's only dew, Harry!' She also loved and took care of many, but she was more pragmatic in her love.

In July of 2006 my father fell and broke his hip. The operation to replace it should have been easy, but he spent six weeks in Mulago Hospital in Kampala and died with his hip still untouched. My parents had always been like a solid dam wall, holding everything together, and now, as they aged, as they were reaching the point of passing on, who was going to do it?

Would we be able to contain the waters? What would happen if we could not? I'd had a nagging feeling for months that a dam was about to burst and the flood would overwhelm us.

But as I reflected on that last week in the hospital, and all the years growing up, as I watched people come in and out of the hospital offering help and comfort, I realised that although I thought my parents did everything on their own, they didn't. Not even my mother, who seemed so self-contained. When she trusted you to take care of things, and when she saw you could manage, she would let go. They were able to because they were part of a family and community that they loved and cared for. And they were cared for in return. I realised that if we held steady, we would be fine.

I spent that last week of my father's life with him and my mother in the hospital, nursing him, together with Estella and our extended family and friends. Maliza, had who struggled with depression for most of her life, had checked herself in to another hospital a couple of weeks before Daddy's fall and the family split up to care for them both. She came home the day before he died.

We had so much support and love it made his passing bittersweet. Ensconced in the community that I belonged to, I drew strength, I felt love, I found a sense of centredness. I was at home. We cared for my father, mother and sister, and when he died we mourned our loss together. When the time came for me to leave Kampala and come back to Cape Town it was numbing because there were few things here that reminded me of my father. I felt, keenly, the sense of uprootedness, of not belonging.

I listened to my mother's rage at the system that had taken her husband and felt helpless living so far away. All these years I had wanted to interview my mother and write about her.

She had lived through the colonial era in Uganda, been one of the first women to go to university, celebrated independence, survived Milton Obote's first regime, Idi Amin, Obote II and Yoweri Museveni's reign. She had taken care of her five children, including two who were disabled and one who battled mental illness, and many other children. She'd completed her BEd degree, almost completed her Master's, and been married for close to 50 years.

Now I felt the urge to write about my life.

In Limbo ...

I picked them up
the broken notes
and sang them
back together,
crooning in a low voice.
And I marvelled
at the beauty
of such brokenness.

And then ...
BOOM.
The song splintered
again.
The notes scattered into the ether
and for a while
I tried

to piece the melody together
find the chords that bound it ...
But somehow
the centre
kept straying
and a sense of
emptiness seeped
in.

Now each note is
tentative
again.
My ears prick up
listening for alarm
bells,
anticipating
another
interruption
from the choirmaster's baton,
afraid to open up
in full voice
in case
this triggers the next
discordant mess.

I am
in limbo
in the nothingness
between notes.

1 *The Hearth*

The hearth am I ... the deep heart of the dwelling.
A pleasant nook for ease and storytelling,
Where friendship's flame shall find a glad renewal
While mirth and kindly chat supply the fuel.

AUTHOR UNKNOWN

Maliza, my eldest sister, was named after my father's mother. Seven years older than me, she is clever, gentle and adventurous in her cooking. She invented a special method of roasting peanuts that became a family treat on special occasions. Estella, the second eldest, was daring as a child – a tomboy and an artist. She was named after my mother's mother. She taught me how to ride a bicycle and climb trees, made beautiful clothes for my paper dolls and made me do many things that I was scared to do. Fay, named after my mother, came next. She was three years older than me and beautiful. She had the thickest, longest, kinkiest hair, a great sense of humour and the most expressive fingers. And when she laughed, we all laughed. Chris, who had my father's first name, came after her. He had the softest, curliest hair that we girls all wished we had. Chris was a charmer and he loved music and dancing. He could find any music station on the radio and knew how to operate the record player.

Last of all there was me. My names are Philippa Anne Namutebi Naluwooza Nalowga Nambuya Mutuwa Muyama Mwihaki – a long story for another time. I was born on the 21st of August 1964 on the sixth floor of New Mulago Hospital. My name was chosen long before I was born. Maama said that one Sunday, when she was a few months pregnant, the preacher had spoken about Philip being love. Something moved within her so if it was a boy, he would be called Philip, and if a girl, Philippa. I was to be their last child. The name Mutuwa is the name given to all last borns, in Lumasaba, my mother's language. The name, Namutebi, identifies me as a member of the Mamba clan of Buganda. Jajja Nuwa Sematimba, my paternal grandfather, gave it to me. Daddy made a card to welcome me into the family and to congratulate Maama. In it he wrote:

Welcome home – Mummy and Philippa
Congratulations
It has been a hard fought battle
And goodbye to
Early morning health exercises
Being an extra strong double carrier!
The delights of backache.
Such delightful sleepless nights.
Balloon dances too.

I was definitely the last.

My father, Henry Barlow, was a civil servant and a poet. He was the eldest son of John and Maliza Barlow and had eight siblings. The name Barlow? My grandfather was the son of a British soldier and a Ugandan woman who we suspect died during childbirth. Unfortunately not much is known about her, as is the case of many women. Jajja John was brought by a missionary, Rev. Walker, to Micah Sematimba, his friend. Sematimba was a prominent Muganda chief who facilitated the safe travel of missionaries across East Africa. Walker carried a letter with him from Cuthbert Lambert Barlow, asking him to care for his son until he was 18, promising to send money for his upkeep and education. At 18 he was to be sent to Cuthbert's brother in Ceylon. For a while after that he sent money and letters.

He never returned and after a while the letters and money stopped coming. Micah and Elizabeth Sematimba loved Jajja John and brought him up as one of their sons, together with Jajja Nuwa, Jajja Drumond and their sisters. They were Jajja John's true family. So we are descendants of Micah Sematimba and Cuthbert Lambert Barlow. While his identity, and that of his progeny, was Baganda, and he was considered a son of Micah Sematimba, he carried his biological father's name, Barlow, because the Baganda are patrilineal. Years after Jajja John died, my Uncle Dennis, Daddy's youngest brother, found out that Cuthbert Lambert Barlow had died in Flanders, Belgium in the First World War. His name is on the war memorial.

My father had a great sense of humour – and a big laugh. He had an incredible ability to laugh at himself – something he tried, with little luck, to teach me to do. I was an earnest child. When he sneezed, he would say a loud 'Bushei!' and Fay would burst into uncontrollable laughter. Daddy always made time for us. He would play high jump in the garden or take us swimming at his friend's house. On our way there, we would stop at the petrol station to pump up the tyre tubes we used to help us float. We would return home, hair kinky and dry, skin grey. Daddy loved gardening, particularly planting flowers. Maama told us that when they were at university he planted flowers outside the window of his room. When she had to do the flower arrangement in chapel, she would go there and get flowers. When we were small, I remember helping create flower beds to plant seedlings. One of my favourite things was going for rides in his car. We would sing and if it was dark and there was a full moon, he would try and race with the moon as we shrieked in the back: 'Faster Daddy, faster!'

My mother, Fayce, was a teacher by profession, a fighter for justice, a wonderful cook, a seamstress and a narrator of stories. She was the eldest daughter of Yokana and Esteri Kutosi, and second eldest child in her family. She too had eight siblings, two of whom died when they were children. Her father was an orphan. His father had left him an inheritance of cattle to use as a dowry when the time was right. He wanted to go to school so he sold them to pay for his education, much to the dismay of his elder half-brother.

Maama was the matriarch and held the family together in her special way. She enjoyed entertaining and both sides of the family remember her family teas and large, delicious lunches. When I was about five, Daddy bought Maama a Kenwood Chef for her birthday. She looked in the recipe book and made us a milkshake using the liquidiser. The recipe needed ice cream and there was no ice cream in the house. Then she remembered that we had strawberry jam, so she made us a milkshake using jam and bananas. We stood around the Kenwood, savouring glasses of pink milk magicked up by my mother and this machine.

Maama was a great storyteller and I sat with her, listening to her tell stories or teach me games. She passed on to me her great love of literature – oral and written. When I was 11, I picked up *Cancer Ward* by Alexander Solzhenitsyn and read it with great determination. She was surprised but she helped me through it. As I grew older, we continued to share books. When I was a teenager, we (Maama, Daddy, Estella and I) read *The Thorn Birds*; *Tell Me That You Love Me, Junie Moon*; *The Secret Diary of Adrian Mole, Aged 13¾* and many more books.

Maama was intellectual and enjoyed a good argument. In her later years she joined a book club, although at first she was frustrated with the level of discussion. She wanted to go into the themes and characterisation. Education, to her, was not an option but a necessity and she facilitated access to education for many members of the extended family – and even strangers.

Like all families, we had our challenges. Both Fay and Chris had cerebral palsy. We never really spoke about what caused it, but Maama told the story of how a year before Fay was conceived she had a miscarriage. That year, Daddy went to Balliol College at Oxford University, to do his postgraduate diploma in agricultural economics, and Maama, Maliza and Estella accompanied him. The doctors who treated her for her miscarriage there discovered that her blood type was O negative. This was a surprise and she became the object of interest because until then these doctors had thought only white people had rhesus negative blood. She was told that when she went home she should inform her doctors as it was important to manage her pregnancies.

But the first Ugandan doctor she told on her return laughed at her and said, 'Olowooz'oli muzungu?[1] Hmmm!', treating her as if she thought one trip to England made her white. I suspect that her subsequent pregnancies with Fay and Chris were not managed appropriately. When I came along, her pregnancy and my birth were managed by a different doctor. My parents gave me his wife's name, Ann, as one of my middle names.

Fay and Chris did not speak, although they understood everything and made sounds to communicate with us. They needed help getting dressed and eating. Many things in our home revolved around their needs. As a child, I did not think much about why they were different; they were simply Fay and Chris. I played with them, I learnt how to communicate with them, to read their body language, their eyes, and ask them questions. If anyone spoke carelessly about them in their presence, as if they were stupid, they got an earful from me, regardless of their age. I knew from the way Fay and Chris laughed at funny things and cried at painful things, that they understood life. They could just not speak or take care of themselves.

We were a close-knit family. Aunts, uncles and cousins were part of our lives and celebrated Christmas, birthdays, weddings and other occasions with us. A cousin, aunt or uncle often stayed with us for short or extended periods. My cousin Joyce, the eldest daughter of Uncle Charles, my mother's brother, was

---

1. Do you think you are a white person?

like an older sister. She lived with us until we left Uganda in 1977. My Aunty Ida, Uncle Dennis, Uncle Patrick, my mother's cousin Salome – they all stayed with us at some point. And people dropped in often. We also visited our grandparents, my father's more often because they lived close by. But I will never forget the visits to my mother's parents.

One Christmas we packed Daddy's beloved old DKW – which we called the Gobodo because of the sound it made as it puttered along the road, and the Volvo, which we called the ovloV because when we sat in the back of the car and looked out of the back windscreen, that is what we saw – and went and spent Christmas in Bukhaweka, with my mother's parents. Daddy drove the Volvo with Maama, and Fay, Chris and me in the back, and Uncle Patrick drove the DKW, with Maliza, Estella, Joyce, Aunty Salome, and all the provisions we needed. The town of Mbale is about 220 kilometres east of Kampala and Bukhaweka is a few kilometres further, closer to the border with Kenya, in the Mount Elgon National Park.

Going through the dense Mabira Forest was exciting. There were parts of the road where you felt as if you were going through a tunnel. As we neared Jinja, the first big town on the trip, we would anticipate going over the Owen Falls Dam, built across the White Nile River. As we drove, to the right you would see the dam, water still like a lake, and to your left, water falling down the high wall, tumbling and crashing into the river that rushed away. Maama would say, 'This is where our electricity comes from!' If we had time, we would stop at the lookout point and gaze at the Nile splashing against the rocks. I always felt a mixture of awe and fear, loving the sound of the water, and fearful of its power and what would happen if

I fell in. It seemed to pull me towards it, so I made sure I stood very, very far from the edge.

Then we got to Tororo Rock as we drove into Tororo town. It's a tall rock formation that can be seen from anywhere in the Tororo district. The town is named after it, and the word means 'place of fog' because the rock is often covered in fog. As we drove into Mbale, Mount Masaba (or Elgon as it is called in the geography books) towered behind the town, reaching into the clouds. We drove over the Manafwa River and finally arrived in Bukhaweka to Khukhu's yellow rice, cooked over a wood fire.

I would sit in her kitchen watching her cook, my eyes tearing up because of the smoke, while she worked dry-eyed. I would watch her smear the floors with cow dung, but she never let me try. When I first saw this, I thought, *How can Khukhu do this with cow poo?* But then Maama told me that the cow dung kept the floors smooth and dust free, and kept away pests such as jiggers, the small fleas that live in the soil and sand. I also learnt that Khukha's house, which was made of mud and wattle, with a thatched roof, was much warmer at night than Uncle's cement and corrugated iron house. So on most visits, that is where we chose to sleep.

I woke up early and brushed my teeth outside, with a cup of water, as the cool mountain air bit into my skin. Then I went with my cousin John to tie the goats in the meadow or fetch water from the stream. When we were thirsty, Khukhu took water from the pot she kept in her room – the coolest, sweetest water.

My parents met at Makerere College in the 1950s. It was then a college of the University of London, later to become one of the best universities in East Africa. Daddy, together with his best friends, ZHK Bigirwenkya and Nathan Bisamunyu, graduated with BAs and were among the first 13 students to be awarded a degree from Makerere. They remained like brothers for the rest of their lives.

Maama received a diploma in education. She did not have the money at the time to get the matriculation exemption, and in those days most women did diplomas. My parents married in 1956 and worked in various parts of Uganda: Mbale, Entebbe and Masaka, and finally settled in Kampala. By the time I came along, my father was a senior civil servant and my mother a teacher. They were part of the circle of young, well-educated and up-and-coming Ugandans with a passion to build their nation. Theirs was a generation committed to family, community and country. They encouraged and enabled many young people to pursue their education.

Kampala in the 1960s was a bustling town. It became a town centre in 1948 and was upgraded to a capital city at independence in 1962. The city was known to have been built on seven hills, but as it is such a hilly city, I never knew which the main hills were, and my seven hills were the ones where I grew up and spent time: Makerere, Kololo, Muyenga, Makindye, Mulago, Kibuli and Nakasero.

Growing up, we lived in Nakasero, and I went to Nakasero Primary School. Kololo was the hill we saw across the valley from the garden of our first home in Kitante Road, and on top of the hill was a towering mast, which we were told made the TV waves travel. Muyenga was beginning to sprout modern homes and my parents built their first house there in 1964. Makerere, home of the oldest university in East Africa, with Wandegeya its neighbouring trading centre, is where my parents met. As a child I had many good friends who lived on campus because their parents worked there. We spent hours running around campus, playing, swimming in the pool and forming firm friendships that continue to this day. Kibuli was a place we often passed on our way to Muyenga or Munyonyo, and its little mosque – one of the oldest in the city – was a landmark.

Kampala has grown extensively since the 1960s. Munyonyo, which is now an upmarket suburb of Kampala, was a village outside of town. Jajja John and Jajja Maliza lived there and I remember driving past many mud-houses with thatched or corrugated iron roofs. Most houses had no electricity and no running water, so they had large tanks that harvested rain-water. Each home had its lusuku (banana garden) and vegetable garden. The lucky ones had a cow or two, and chickens scratch-ing around. People took care of their compounds; they were always well swept and neat. The Jajjas had a number of cows, a large lusuku and 11 mango trees – one for each of their nine children and themselves. Visiting during the mango season was delicious fun. We would climb the trees and pick the juiciest mangos, eat most of the flesh, then suck the juice out of the remaining fibrous flesh until the hair was standing up. These would become the heads of the dolls we would make; the bodies would be made from the bark of a banana tree.

When I was growing up, the central shopping district was on Kampala Road, with department stores like Drapers and Nelsadry's. Further along was everyone's favourite bakery – Christo's. Cakes and pies for special occasions. French loaves and sausage rolls.

When I was in P3, my third year of primary school, I had

recorder lessons with Mrs Giovanni on a Tuesday over lunchtime. In those days we used to go home for lunch; there were no traffic jams. On Tuesdays we brought packed lunch and this one day Maama said Badru, the driver, would bring me lunch. As soon as class ended, I ran outside to the waiting area, and there was Badru with a box from Christo's. I smelt them long before I opened the box – warm sausage rolls with flaky pastry that peeled off. I could have died with joy.

Further down Kampala Road was the Norman Cinema – what is now the Watoto Church – where I watched *Blackbeard's Ghost* and many other movies. Across the road was an Indian shop where we bought sweetmeats – penda and barfi na mawa. Almost diagonally opposite was Happy Tots, where we got our Start-rite shoes – smart and comfortable, with that special leather smell.

Many streets down the hill was the Nakasero Market – clean, organised, busy and noisy. Women, mostly, sat at their stalls with oranges, bright red tomatoes, pawpaws as big as someone's head and pineapples just a little bit smaller. There were all sorts of greens: spinach, ebugga and doodo; nakati; lettuce and cabbage. And all kinds of bananas: matooke, bundizi, gonja and bogoya. It was here that Maama bought vegetables, fruit, and meat. Like most people, she built relationships with the tradeswomen, and had her favourites who gave her good deals and fresh produce. I was terrified of the men who walked around carrying heavy sacks on their backs, shouting for people to move out of their way.

Next to the market was Jaffries, the ice cream parlour, and if I did not complain about the long wait in the market while Maama bargained, I would soon be licking a creamy cone. Or sometimes she would buy potato crisps from the supermarket. The crisps came unsalted, so we fished in the packet for the cone-shaped paper of salt and sprinkled it over the crisps.

On the other side of town was the busy railway station – a grand place. We knew it well. My mother's brother, Uncle Charles, worked at the Kilembe Mines, and so we often took my cousin Joyce to the station when she was going home for holidays – or went there to fetch her. I remember watching her step onto the train, envious, and dying to travel like Joyce. The whistle would blow and it would start moving – *chigi chigi, chigi chigi* – and Joyce would stick her head out of the window and wave. We would sing our song, 'Chu chu traini weeraba, chu chu traini weeraba', and wave back.

Up the road from the station, opposite the Parliament buildings, was the National Theatre, where locally written plays, school drama and music festivals, and even national drama festivals were held. I went with my mother to watch *Oluyimba lwa Wankoko*, a musical in Luganda by Byron Kawadwa, and *Renga Moi* by Robert Serumaga. Both plays were commentaries on Uganda in the 1970s.

I'd sit in the greenroom with my father and poets, artists and activists such as David Rubadiri and Pio and Elvania Zirimu, listening to poetry and play readings. Once I recited the poem I had learnt at school for a competition – 'I think mice are rather nice, their tails are long ...' – and they clapped.

Opposite the National Theatre was Dewinton Street, where we bought apples, grapes, and Jaffa oranges from Israel. There was a restaurant called Sardinias, which is still in exactly the same place today and owned by the same Chinese family since 1971. They sold Chinese and Indian food. There were many days we begged Maama for a Sardinias' samosa. I can still recall the aroma drifting out of the doorway.

On the other side of Parliament was City Hall, which housed a public library. I loved reading and Maama enrolled me there. I would go and check out books by Enid Blyton and, in later years, the Nancy Drew stories and the Bobbsey Twins series, as well as more Enid Blyton: the Malory Towers and St Clare's series. Then I would sit under a grand old tree waiting for Maama. That tree is still there.

In primary school we did not have many books written by African writers, or that had characters who looked and lived like us. Apart from folktales, and a few stories in English comprehension books, I read my first truly Ugandan book when I was about 11 or 12. My generation loved the Moses series by Barbara Kimenye, a writer who identified as Ugandan. She wrote about Moses and his friend Itchy-Fingers and their escapades at Mukiibi's Educational Institute for the Sons of African Gentlemen. In secondary school we read books and poems by the likes of Ngugi wa Thiong'o, Okot p'Bitek, Robert Serumaga, John Ruganda, Chinua Achebe, Wole Soyinka and Ama Ata Aidoo, among others.

National holidays were a big distraction and we celebrated them with much pomp and ceremony. On Independence Day there were floats along Kampala Road. We lined the streets and stood on the balconies of buildings. In the evening, there were fireworks on the Kololo Airstrip. There was a bandstand in the gardens next to the Apollo Hotel, where a band sometimes performed on a Sunday afternoon. Around Christmas, the tallest Christmas tree I had ever seen would be lit in those gardens, and we sang carols, with the band playing in the bandstand.

Then there was the drive-in cinema in Ntinda. The DKW had a giant boot and on drive-in nights my parents put a mattress in the back. Maama cooked a big dish of chips, deep-fried gonja and pork sausages, which we took along. The first movie I watched there was *Cinderella*.

On the 9th of October 1962, Uganda gained its independence from the British. I had always believed that, in my earliest years, Uganda was peaceful, that we had had a smooth transition from the colonial era, and that the trouble only started with Idi Amin. Looking back, I now see the cracks in the very foundations of our independence, which made Uganda's journey inevitably rocky.

Uganda was a British protectorate. There were no settlers. While the locals had more freedom than the Kenyans or South Africans, there were still structures that frustrated their growth and kept the economic and political power in the hands of the Europeans and Indians. Although racism was not legislated in the colonial period, there are records to show that Africans were regarded as third-class citizens. While Africans could grow cotton, they were not allowed to gin – to separate the cotton fibre from the seeds – or to market it. This was the domain of the Europeans and Asians. Few, if any, Africans could go into the wholesale business because the law required wholesalers to own a concrete building, and in those days few Africans did.

The push for independence seems to have come out of two impulses – from the Farmers' Unions, which were agitating for a better deal, and from the young Ugandan intellectuals who won scholarships to study in Britain and who travelled abroad. Through their education, they began to see new possibilities, and began to agitate for them. Some of them lost their scholarships before they finished their courses because the colonial government considered them to be a threat. My father's uncle, Ignatius Musaazi, was one of those. He went on to start the first political party in Uganda – the Uganda National Congress. In 1945 and 1949 there were riots in Buganda. In 1949 the people burnt the homes of the Buganda chiefs who supported the colonial government. They demanded that the government remove the controls on the prices of export cotton sales, that Africans be allowed to gin cotton and that the common man have representation in the local government, instead of the local chiefs.

Sir John Hall, who was then governor, ignored these riots, casting them as being instigated by 'communists'. But the world was changing. India got its independence in 1947 and in West Africa things were also changing. In 1952, a new governor, Andrew Cohen, came into power and he began to listen to Ugandan demands and implement some of them. He removed the restrictions on African cotton ginning, took away the price controls on Ugandan coffee grown by Africans, encouraged the establishment of cooperatives and established the Uganda Development Corporation to promote and finance new projects. The Uganda Legislative Council was also reorganised to include African representatives elected from districts throughout Uganda.

There were many people who played important roles in the lead-up to independence. They were all working towards a common goal but they had ideological differences. The Buganda loyalists were pushing for a federal government, which would give Buganda significant concessions. There were those who were pushing for one nation; those who were pushing for a socialist state; those pushing for a more capitalist state;

there were those who used the ethnic and religious divisions for their own purposes; and those who tried to build bridges across these divisions. Sometimes these differences were deeply buried in order to achieve the common goal – but they were still alive under the surface.

On the eve of independence in 1962, after much political manoeuvring, the fragile alliance between the Uganda People's Congress (UPC), led by Obote, and the Buganda-led Kabaka Yekka party, was poised to govern the country in a coalition. The new constitution favoured Buganda over the western kingdoms of Toro, Ankole and Bunyoro – giving the Kingdom of Buganda semi-federal status, but offering little to the other kingdoms. This caused consternation. Kabaka Muteesa II of Buganda was installed as ceremonial president and Milton Obote of the UPC was installed as prime minister. Their visions for Uganda were not aligned.

It wasn't long before the alliance between the UPC and KY broke up, resulting in Obote suspending the constitution and appointing himself as president in 1966. In response, Kabaka and his parliament asked Obote to remove his government from Buganda. Obote retaliated by commanding the army to storm the palace of Kabaka Muteesa, who fled to the United Kingdom, where he died in exile in 1969.

By 1969 Obote had banned all other political parties, imprisoned many who opposed him and declared his Move to the Left – a road map to socialism, largely influenced by Julius Nyerere's Ujamaa policy in Tanzania. In December 1969 there was an attempted assassination and in 1971 Amin came to power.

Looking back over the history of my motherland, I have learnt that, even then, love and hate, peace and unrest, hope and disillusionment, prejudice and respect lived side by side. Our parents did all they could to give us the best possible life and to protect us. I can see now that it is not easy to shelter children from what is happening around them. One of my earliest memories of political unrest was of me in a Land Rover outside Mulago hospital. It kept returning over the years. I never got round to asking my mother if she remembered what had been happening at the time. Months after she passed away, as I sorted out her things, I found index cards where she had written about the incident. I turned them into poems.

At the gates of Mulago: I

December 1969
There was nothing
extraordinary about
that night
when my husband and I
went to bed
in our suburban house
on Kitante Road.

Nothing
until ...
At 1am
the staccato of gunfire
ruptured the night skies
waking us.

We did not sleep again.

Morning came
grey and wet
and strangely silent,
a feeble sun straining
through the clouds

The news filtered through.
On the radio.
The President had been shot
in the jaw.
He lay in Mulago Hospital.
Stable.

As I contemplated the day
lightning streaked the sky,
the rumbling in my tummy echoed
the rumbling of the distant thunder.
This was the morning I had to take
our little one to Mulago Hospital

For another measles shot.

My husband held me close.
'I'll send the driver
to take you.'

I sat next to my child

in the front cab of the Land Rover
the roar of the engine
louder with each gear change,
diesel fumes filling the cab.
And outside,
people walked.
Bodies strangely taut,
eyes darting from side to side
as if expecting
another shower
of gunfire.

We stopped at the entrance
one of the gates
ripped off its hinges.

On the ground
two men lay
bodies twisted grotesquely.
'They are dead,' said the driver.

My little one stood up,
looked at the bodies silently.
I gently turned her head away and
drew her close.

As we drove in
through the hospital gates
a Black Maria police van
arrived to take the bodies away.

At the gates of Mulago: II

December 1969
Five years old
sitting next to Maama
in the front of a Land Rover.
Going for a shot,
I must be brave.

The ride is
big, noisy, bumpy, smelly...
not like Maama's car.

We stop at the hospital gates.
My heart beats faster.

Outside the big people
talk in loud, short bursts.
I hear no smiles, no greetings.
My heart wants to run away.

I stand up and look out,
policemen with guns.
No smiles on their faces.

A man
twisted on the ground.
Another, not so far away.

'They're dead,' says the driver
to Maama.

A coldness in my tummy.
I look at the big people.
Their hearts are beating faster too,
I think.

Maama pulls me back
into my seat
closer to her,
and we drive in
through the gates.

At the gates of Mulago: III

December 1969
Two ward maids talked
in the corridor.
As I walked past
with my little one's hand in mine,
I heard one say

     'Those two men
     who were shot at the gate,'

I stopped nearby to listen.

'They came in last night.
They had brought a woman
to deliver.'

'Really? At Maternity?'

I looked down at my child
and listened on.

'Mbu the husband,
anti he was a lorry driver,
told the wife nti he must take
the turn-boy back to the lorry.'

'And then?'

'The wife said, "Don't go now.
Can't you hear those gun shots?
Bwe pa pa pa pa pa!
Stay until the sun comes out, please!"'

'Bannange!'

I picked up my little one
eyes opened wide, brow creased
as she looked on.

'Mbu the man said, "We must go.
We have to look after
the things in the lorry.

The boss doesn't know
we are here.'"

'Eh, eh – these men! And so they went?'
'Hmm.
And after the baby was born
someone came in and told them
that the men had been shot.'

'Bannange, nga Kitalo!'[2]

'Kitalo nnyo,' I said.
'It is a terrible loss indeed.'

And as they walked away
I hugged my child closer,
prayed for that mother
and her baby,
and thought about the
ordinary night that
in a moment changed
so many lives.

This is the backdrop against which my story began.

My earliest memory of home is the house on plot no. 13 Kitante
Road, Kampala: an old colonial house with a large front garden

---

2. Oh my goodness, what a terrible loss!

cushioning it from the busy road. Terracotta roof tiles, creamy white walls, with a band of black paint wrapped around the bottom, to keep off the splash of red soil when it rained. Double-storied with high ceilings and wooden floors. The front had a spacious veranda, enclosed in burglar proofing and mosquito netting, keeping it cool. Doors led off to the garden on both ends of the veranda. We played many games here. It was the children's domain, where our wooden toybox was housed.

The lounge was the adults' space. The TV and the Grundig phonogram – the radio and record player that looked like a sideboard – were in that room and when the parents were away, we would play in the lounge and then tidy up quickly before they came home. In the lounge there was a wooden staircase leading to three bedrooms and a bathroom. Sometimes, when we were sent to bed, we would climb up noisily, stomping our feet, and then creep down quietly to listen to the conversation or the TV.

We had a spacious garden at the front and back. The front garden was dotted with fruit trees. Daddy's favourite was an orange tree in front of the kitchen, with the sweetest oranges in the world. In the front, close to the driveway, the majestic ffene tree gave shade, sweet, pungent jackfruit and leaves to make stick helicopters. We loved the jackfruit. Daddy hated the smell, so when the fruit was ripe, we cut it open and ate it at the bottom of the garden. There were three guava trees and a loquat tree too.

Close to these trees at the bottom of the garden was the swing, a wooden slat with ropes on either side. I stood on it and swung higher and higher by bending my knees at the right moment. At the very bottom of the garden was my favourite space, a bougainvillea bush growing close to the fence, arching onto the hedge and creating a passageway to play in.

Our neighbours on the one side were the Kamwakas. They were Ugandans. The children were mostly older than me, except for Simon, who I sometimes played with. Their father worked in the Ministry of Information and we sometimes went over to watch documentaries in the evening. On the other side there was an Italian family with two boys. Alberto, the older one, and I spent many happy hours together. Next to them was an English family with two girls, Sarah and Miranda. We didn't get on with them.

Across the road were the golf course and the Kitante valley that climbed up to Kololo Hill. If you looked carefully, you could see Aunty Lerlynn and Uncle George's house in Kololo. Sometimes we would see their car, small as an ant, driving out or returning home.

Kitante was a safe and carefree neighbourhood, with hedges, not fences, between the houses. We played across each other's compounds, and in the valley, returning home just before dusk. One of our favourite games was walking along the water pipes at the bottom of the valley, behind the Golf Club and close to Acacia Avenue. A long walk for me, but I followed Estella and was determined to get up the courage and balance to walk across the pipes without having to sit down in fear. Sometimes we would go fishing for tadpoles in the drains that ran through the golf course.

When our cousins came we performed concerts for our parents, and collected money at the end for sweets.

The extravaganza

The adults sit
upright on dining room chairs
in sitting room turned concert hall.
The staircase
a dark wooden backdrop
to the stage.

Someone welcomes them.
Item number 1:
All the children
singing and dancing
Norah's Indian song.

'Mwogowali mali mali
Mwogowali maaaali
Eeeeva pali, teeeva pali
Chakara, chakara
Shugari shari.'

Foreign words
that were probably incorrect,
hand and leg movements
imperfect,
faces beaming.

Next – Joyce's song.
Choir in place,

hands together
and
'Sikwendera, sikwendera
sipiriti, sipiriti, sikwendera, sikwendera
oh sipiriti!
Oh, oh, oh sipiriti'

The parents clap,
the performers
move on with glee
to
the finale
the bakisimba dance
White enamel basin now
a throbbing drum.
'Olunkutiza, olunkutiza
olunkutiz'olukutwala mu
bakisimba ...'[3]

Dancers in line.
Sweaters on hips.
The singers start:
'Twe yanze twe yanze,
waalalala kabweteme mu mwonger'ekyupa
Nabulagala ...'

---

3. The Baganda use spoken rhythms to teach people to play the drums
that accompany their singing and dance music. This is the rhythm played
on the bakisimba drum.

Dancers march in, kneel down.
Clasped hands move left,
clasped hands move right
and then …
they stand.
Hips swivel
this way and that,
feet stepping
steady to the beat,
singing, clapping, and ululating.
The audience joins in.

The basin-drum climaxes

Tu tu tu!
Tu tu, tu tu
Tu Tu Tu
Tu Tu Tu
Tu PA!

The concert ends.
Eyes shining
the hat is passed round
the sweet promise of tomorrow.

Sometimes the visitors were more senior members of the family. In Luganda we call our grandparents Jajja and then we add their name. It's a unisex term, so my father's father was Jajja John and his mother was Jajja Maliza. All their brothers and sisters we also called Jajja. They both came from large families, particularly Jajja Maliza. And you never asked an older person who they were – you were expected to know them. One of the people who fascinated me was Jajja Ewumeri, one of my father's aunts. I will never forget the first time I met her:

Jajja Ewumeri

Home from school
at lunchtime
we walk into
the sitting room
and find
three old ladies
sitting there.

We kneel down
and greet them
one by one.

'Mummanyi?'[4]
asks the one with
sparkling eyes.
We are silent.
If we say yes,
we will have to explain who she is.
If we say no, we will be rude.

---

4. Do you people know who I am?

Someone brings her a
glass of ice.
She crunches it
like sweets.
My eyes open wide,
my lips curl upwards.
Everyone else fades into the background.
Jajja looks at Maliza
and asks 'Aani ono?'
Who is this one?
My eyes grow bigger.
as her
lower lip stretches
like a pointing finger.

Aunty Irene
introduces each one of us.

I only have eyes
for the Jajja
whose finger-lip conducts
the conversations.
We soon find out
she is Daddy's aunt.

I met her again
at my father's funeral.
I was all grown up
with children of my own.

Her eyes still sparkled.

I sat with her
as we remembered my father.
And then I asked,
'Jajja, okyalya ayisi?'
Grandma, do you still eat ice?
She looked at me
smiled wide and toothless
and shook her head.
'Nedda mwana wange,
amanyo sikyalina!'[5]
But her mouth still points.

Family and friends who were often in our home learnt quickly that Fay and Chris were at the heart of our household. We ate with them, I bathed with them, and I shared all my early birthday parties with them too. I realise now that although Daddy bought Maama the Kenwood Chef as a birthday present, it was also necessary to liquidise food for Fay and Chris, and to mince their meat. As soon as she unpacked it, she made something for all of us to share, so it became ours. It took me a long time to find the words to explain what I intuitively understood, probably around the age of five, that they were different from most people, and we loved them as much, or more. They were like our unconventional Christmas trees – not firs like everyone else's, but beautiful all the same.

---

5. No my child. I don't have many teeth left.

Fay

Christmas time.
It must have been.
For the dry tree-like branch that Daddy had found
was decorated with baubles galore,
standing tall in the corner.

There on a sofa
was Fay
with a pipe in her nose
doll on her lap.

Maama put a syringe
in the pipe.
Creamy, white
liquid food
travelled up, into Fay's nose.

The tree behind me,
eyes on Maama.
I shuffled toe by toe
towards the sofa.
As Maama put down the syringe,
fingers touched the edge of the sofa
bum slowly inched on.
Leaning back, next to her, I said

'Look Fay.
It's the Christmas tree.'

At any time of the year in Kitante Road, you would find the neighbourhood children playing at each other's houses. One day I was in our back garden with Sarah, one of the English girls who lived next to Alberto. We weren't friends although we sometimes shared lifts to school. Under the big kabaka anjagala, the candlenut tree, we got into a fight, and being a tomboy I was winning. Miranda, Sarah's big sister, found us. Miranda was at least a head taller than us. She pushed me to the ground, face down, and then sat on top of me, pinching me on each arm. I couldn't move so I screamed as loudly as I could and Estella, my sister, and Norah, my cousin, came to the rescue.

Norah took nonsense from no one. She grabbed Miranda, threw her aside, picked me up and passed me on to Estella, who helped me dust myself off. Norah stared down at Miranda, hands on hips, eyes flashing and said. 'If you ever touch my cousin again, you will see.'

Miranda stood up, ears red, and said, 'But, but, but …'

Norah said, 'But WHAT?' Miranda kept quiet. Then Norah turned around and said, 'Wama Philippa, tugende.' She took my hand and we marched off. Norah was forever my hero.

My parents had many Indian friends. One Saturday morning, Babu, one of Daddy's close friends, came for a visit. I was out in the garden playing. Daddy and Babu stood under a tree talking. Babu was a tall man, with dark brown skin, darker than Daddy's. His hair was jet black and so were his eyes. Babu beckoned to me and I went up to him, hoping for a packet of sweets.

Instead he gave me a small transistor radio. He said, 'This child is clever. I want her to have this radio.' I am not sure what else he said. I was excited and proud – he thought I was clever. When Maama came outside, I ran up to her to show her my gift.

My mother was an interesting mixture of someone who sometimes stepped beyond what tradition expected of her but who also held strong traditional views. She smiled and said, 'Thank you Babu. You are very kind, but this is not a toy for a young child' (or something like that) and she gave it to Maliza, my eldest sister. I was heartbroken.

I felt, in that moment, that my mother did not want me to be as clever as my big sister. I sometimes wonder if I have carried that belief deep inside me all my life.

For a long time, I refused to listen to the news on the radio.

It was a Sunday. We were having guests for lunch. The house was full of noise and activity. Someone was vacuum cleaning, the tables were being polished and dusted, someone else was cleaning Maama's favourite cutlery and china. The smells from the kitchen – roast chicken and potatoes; succulent fillet; binyebwa ni kamaleeya (groundnut sauce with smoked bamboo shoots, a delicacy from my mother's part of the world) – filled the air, stirring my salivary glands. Wherever I went in the house I heard, 'Not here, Philippa! Why don't you go outside and play? But *don't* climb any trees, or get your clothes dirty.'

Maama had invited a Russian lady to lunch. I had no idea what Russians were, but clearly this was an important day. The car drove up the driveway and out came Maama, Daddy and a woman. She was much taller than Maama and her skin was almost white. She spoke English with a strong accent. This was the woman Maama had met when she went to Russia as part of a Ugandan delegation. The strongest memory Maama had was that they could not do anything on their own. As soon as they stepped out of the hotel to explore, someone appeared either to walk with them or to take them back to the rest of the group. This one woman had been intrigued when Maama told her that in Uganda you could go anywhere alone. Maama promised to invite her home for a meal if she ever came to Uganda.

In Uganda the Russian delegation was under close scrutiny but Maama and Daddy had somehow managed to sneak the woman away from the Apollo Hotel (what is now the Sheraton) and bring her home. There was an intensity about that afternoon, charged by the secrecy of what they were doing. It was considered wrong, but it was so right. The lady talked and laughed and got to know each of us. She brought some red matryoshka dolls. She slowly opened the big one and out came another, and then another and then another. It was like magic. I spent time playing with them and later those matryoshka dolls stood in various places of honour in all the homes we lived in.

After lunch, Maama and Daddy took the lady back to her hotel. She was laughing. After she returned to Russia, Maama never heard from her again. She prayed that nothing terrible had happened to her but was always glad that she had followed her heart and invited her over.

2 *Stoking the fire*

Wood already touched by fire is not hard to set alight.
AFRICAN PROVERB

On Sundays we went to All Saints Church, Daddy in his dark suit and tie, Maama in her dress, low heels with matching handbag – sometimes wearing a wig. The girls wore short dresses, legs covered in white knee-length socks ending in our nice 'church shoes.' Chris in his smart shorts, short-sleeved shirt, grey knee-length socks and his specially made shoes. Fay and Chris would have bibs on because they sometimes drooled. My parents made a conscious decision not to hide Fay and Chris – as was the practice in many families in those days. Disability, in most communities, was taboo. Given my parents' apparent ease with their disabled children, people often came to speak to them about their own disabled children.

Maama and Daddy realised that Fay and Chris, and many

other children, needed more care and support than was available in a conventional school setting, so together with a few other parents they helped start the Uganda Spastic Society and the Kampala School for the Physically and Mentally Handicapped in early 1966. The school's first premises were a storeroom at Mengo Primary School. Then it moved to a house on the land that Kabaka Muteesa II, the King of Buganda, had given them.

A school with classrooms, dormitories and vocational workshops was built on the plot next to the headmaster's house. The students who did not proceed to secondary school were taught trades such as tailoring and carpentry and, in later years, the art of fabric dyeing, and bead making. There were also many activities at the school to which the public were invited: concerts, fêtes and open days to show what these young people could achieve. One boy at the school, Mukasa, was a charmer. Mukasa had a condition where his arms, legs and torso did not grow. He needed help doing almost everything but he had a strong, powerful voice and a smile that made you see the person beyond his disabilities. Mukasa moved around on a cart, made out of a pram, I think. I looked forward to his performances at the concerts – his rich voice made me feel like all was well. Mukasa did not live long but he lived a full life and touched many others.

The children at the school loved Fay and Chris. Once, when we went to fetch them, a boy with the biggest smile walked out of class with us. The teacher asked him what he was doing and he said, 'Mperekera Fureyi ne Gurisi wange' (I am accompanying my 'Fureyi' and 'Gurisi').

Fay and Chris went to school every day and for physiotherapy a few times a week at Mengo Hospital, close to the school. Sometimes I would accompany them. The physiotherapist was

Miss Bremner. She worked with them in a big room that had all sorts of equipment in it. She would get them to walk, holding bars. During one particular session, she rolled Chris on a big ball and helped him walk between two rails. I wanted to be rolled on the big ball. To five-year-old me, it looked like so much fun.

After Amin took over, many expatriates left – Mr Lane, the headmaster of the school, and Miss Bremner too. Not many physiotherapists remained. The teachers and the staff found it easier to work with children who had physical disabilities – there wasn't much available in terms of training for teachers and carers of children with cerebral palsy, and so Fay and Chris stopped going to school. My parents remained involved in the school, on the board, and helping when they could. We took Fay and Chris to concerts and fêtes for the first few years. Those students who showed academic ability were encouraged to further their education in mainstream schools. Many went on to tertiary institutions.

My parents remained connected to the school till the end of their lives. When my father died, the Old Boys and Old Girls Association of the school put an announcement in the newspapers even before we as a family did. At my mother's funeral a young man, now an accountant, told Estella that it was Maama who supported him and encouraged him to continue his education beyond primary school. She encouraged him to persevere when he found the secondary school not built to cater for people with disabilities. When he passed his O Levels, she helped him find a college. We have heard many such testimonies.

I went to Newfield Nursery School in the late 1960s. It was opposite the All Saints Church, now Cathedral, in Nakasero and was run by the church. It stood on the plot where the new church building is now being built. We wore blue dresses with yellow trim round the sleeves and neckline. Maama thought it was rather dull so she sewed a piece of yellow zigzag binding onto my dress. It grew out of my pocket like the stem of a flower, ending on my shoulder. It had a zigzag leaf, but no petals. I loved that uniform. I was so proud when, during an assembly, I was called up for all to see.

Every week, we took a bottle of Ribena, a blackcurrant cordial popular in those days, and Marie biscuits to school. At breaktime the teachers gave us a biscuit and a cup of juice. Before we ate, we would line up to wash our hands, tapping the shoulders of the child in front, singing, 'Hurry up-a, hurry up-a.'

Justa worked at the school. He was tall and strong. I think he might have been a handyman or a janitor. We loved Justa because he played with us. At breaktime we lined up in front of him, waiting for a chance to be picked up, thrown up in the air and caught. We squealed in delight. He had a bright smile, a warm laugh and always made time to play with us.

Sometimes, on a Friday morning the whole school walked up past the church across the road. There was a valley with footpaths that ran through it. It went down to Kyadondo Road, and across from there was the sports field for Nakasero Primary School. We lay down at the top, near the church side, and rolled down the hill into the valley. That was one of my favourite activities – that and the Christmas party.

One year, we sat on the veranda waiting for Father Christmas, thinking every sound was him. Was he coming on a sleigh? But there was no snow. Would he fly through the sky? But how? Then we heard the ringing of the fire engine's siren. It came down the driveway, and out came Father Christmas, in a suit as red as the fire engine. He had a huge bag slung over his shoulder. He took a few of us for a short ride on his Christmas engine.

Newfield remains indelibly marked in my heart for other reasons, too.

The Caregiver

12.30 the
school bell rings.
Some children run,
straight into their mother's arms.
The rest sit on the veranda and wait.
One by one the children go,
then all the teachers too.
I am left alone
with the caregiver.

She looks at me
sitting beside her on the cement floor,
clutching my school bag.
My brown eyes scour the road
for Daddy's car.
'Bakwerabidde.'
They have forgotten you,
she says.

I look straight ahead
pretending I do not understand
the only language I knew
when I started school
that year.

Daddy, please come,
I silently implore.

'Kankusibire mu kyi biina.
Tebajja kukyima leero.'
Let me lock you in the classroom.
They won't fetch you today.

I edge away from her,
looking at the road
praying that each passing car
is coming for me.

'Jangu,' she says.
'Nze nina gyendaga.
Teri anaakunona. Bakwerabidde.'
Come
I have somewhere to go.
No one will fetch you.
They have forgotten you.

She stands up.
I start to hum a tune
as I plan my escape.

Then a grey Saab stops
at the top of the driveway.
The door opens
and out steps Uncle David
in full police uniform.
I grab my bag
run and wrap my arms
around his legs.

The year before I turned six, I left Newfield Nursery. Since I was
born in August, Maama said I might only be allowed to start primary school a year later. I wanted to start that January like all my
friends. Maama took me for two interviews. The first was at the
Kampala Kindergarten. The idea was that I would spend time
there until I was old enough to go to primary school. It seemed
to be a nice place but I wanted to go to big school.

Later Maama took me for an interview at Nakasero Primary
School where my big sisters and cousins were. We drove
through the imposing gates and turned left to the lower school,
where the P1 and P2 classes were. We were led to the P1 classrooms. I sat outside with Maama, heart beating, trying not to
fiddle, until we were called in. She left me in the classroom with
a couple of other children and the teacher. I did activities at
various tables – puzzles and colouring in, and then the teacher
called me up to her desk. She asked me a few questions, then
she pulled out a book and asked me to read. I saw my dream
of primary school slip away before my eyes. I looked at her and
said, 'But I can't read!'

She smiled and said, 'Don't worry. Look at the pictures and

tell me what the book is about.' We had the most wonderful conversation but I left thinking they would not have me yet.

I was so relieved when Maama told me that I had been accepted at Nakasero. I was even prouder when she bought me the uniform. The dress made from green and white checked material, a white collar, buttons down the front of the bodice and belts that tied back at the waist; a dark green cardigan; white ankle socks and a pair of new brown Start-rite shoes from Happy Tots – the best shoe shop on Kampala Road. I was at Big School.

We were still living at no. 13 Kitante Road when Idi Amin came to power. We woke up on the 25th of January 1971 to the sound of gunshots. Maama and Daddy always listened to the news before they did anything else, so they came and told us there had been a coup. I did not understand what that meant. All I understood was that we would not be going to school. Estella and I went upstairs to jump on the wooden floors mimicking the gunshots to scare Maama. Maama came upstairs and gave us a mouthful.

Maama and Daddy kept the radio on all day. There were long interludes of martial music interrupted by announcements that I did not understand. That afternoon, I watched cars driving down Kitante Road, with music blaring, and a pick-up truck with drummers and singers on the back of it singing. People were celebrating the end of Obote's era.

Soon after Amin's coup that January, we moved to 1A Kafu Road, a few blocks away. Just before the coup, Daddy had been appointed as the managing director of the Lint Marketing Board, and this house was part of the job. It was a modern house and had a big black gate, with a fence all around the property. In the driveway was an oval roundabout with a garden in the middle of it. There was a double garage that we would later use as our birthday party space. The garage led into the study where, in later years, we kept the piano that we had inherited from our cousins, the Bigirwenkyas, when they left Uganda.

The front door was French windows, leading into a parlour. The study was to the right. To the left was a sitting room that could take two lounge suites and it led onto a covered veranda that walked round part of the house. A visitor's wing with a bedroom and bathroom had a separate entrance. Off the parlour was the dining room leading into a kitchen with two pantries and a scullery. Upstairs was the master suite, two bedrooms and a bathroom, as well as a study with a balcony. The staff quarters had three or four rooms.

All our bedrooms were upstairs. Fay, Chris and I shared a bedroom. Maliza and Estella shared the other room. There was also a lounge-like room that was Maama's study and sewing room. She began her master's when we moved here. Maama's study had a tiny balcony. The wall was made of brickwork, with gaps in it, and on the other side was the flat roof of the garage.

Estella used to climb over the balcony, onto the roof, and sit under the shade of the mango tree at the end of the house. I always copied Estella in whatever she did, so I tried, but I was too small and scared to climb. However, we discovered that I could climb through the small window above Maama's desk. That became our secret, until Maama asked about the 'monkeys' that were climbing into the house through the window. We feigned innocence until she took us to her desk and showed us the foot and fingerprints on the window sill. That did not stop us from climbing, though. And it came in handy.

One afternoon, during the school holidays, Chris went into our parents' room and locked himself inside. He could not open the door. Both my parents were at work. We tried to get him to open the door but he couldn't, and the key was stuck in the lock. I remembered the small window that opened onto the roof, so I climbed through Maama's study window, onto the roof, walked across to the bathroom window, pulled it open and climbed through. I found Chris looking out of the bedroom window onto the road, watching out for Maama's car. 'Chris,' I said. He turned and looked at me, mouth turned downwards, lips quivering. I walked over to him and we hugged.

My mother always said, 'If someone bullies you, stand up and fight for yourself. Don't let them get away with it. I will support you.' Well, one day in my second year at primary school I tested her words.

During breaktime I was walking around the playground looking for someone to play with. I bumped into my friend Pat. She was in the other P2 class. I slapped her on the arm to say 'Hi', like I always did, and she burst into tears and ran away. I stood there frowning. What had I done? Just then I looked up. Five girls from her class surrounded me. They circled around me saying: 'How could you do that to Pat?' 'Don't you know how painful a cholera injection is?' 'Why did you make her cry?'

I tried to defend myself, to explain, but no one listened. Then they pushed and shoved me – or maybe I tried to break free from the circle that had enclosed me. They pushed me back so I started to fight. Now, I had spent a lot of time playing with boys. In P1 Cowboys and Indians and Cops and Robbers were much more interesting than playing Witches and Fairies. So I kicked back, hit out and pulled.

Then I heard the sound of material tearing. I looked up to see Elizabeth's uniform torn at the waist where the bodice and skirt were sewn together. Elizabeth started crying. And then she saw Miss Kajumba, the head of the lower school, coming onto the playground with the bell.

Elizabeth ran towards her. I disappeared behind a bush. My friend Danny came and asked me what was going on and I told him. He asked if I needed help and I said, 'It is fine, but I think Elizabeth is going to tell Miss Kajumba.' We stood and watched her.

At that moment Miss Kajumba rang the first bell. We all had to stand still and keep quiet. Even Elizabeth who was close enough to speak. Then she rang the second bell, which meant that we had to run and line up in our class lines. Elizabeth went to speak to Miss Kajumba, who replied, 'I don't like tattle tales, Elizabeth, just get into your line.' I was so relieved. I had survived this.

A few days later my parents held a dinner party. We were always allowed to stay up and say hello to the guests. Maama was talking to a well-dressed lady and she beckoned to me and said, 'Philippa, come and meet Elizabeth's mother.' I could have died. Elizabeth's mother started talking about the incident. She went on to tell us how terrible it was, especially since it was a brand new uniform. I explained what had happened and before Elizabeth's mother could say anything more, my mother said: 'You know, one of her older sisters had a friend who always took her breaktime snack in pre-school. From that day on, I have always told my girls that they must stand up for themselves. I am sure she did not mean to tear Elizabeth's uniform but she had to protect herself. Philippa, please apologise.' I said sorry, ran upstairs having had enough of the party, and thanked God for my mother. It was then that I was certain she had my back.

In P1 and P2, we did not have afternoon school, so we would go home at lunchtime. I would get into all sorts of mischief so my mother enrolled me in an after-school programme. That way they could drop me as they took Estella back to school after lunch.

The Great Escape

Finally in BIG school
we were enrolled
for after-school activities
at a kindergarten.

I sat next to her
both of us
rolling our eyes and pouting
as we painted more
baby pictures.

At breaktime we
sat together in a corner
whispering and laughing
and keeping quiet

when someone joined us.
Our eyes sparkled as we waved
goodbye to each other.
'See you tomorrow,' we said.

The next day
at breaktime
while the others played
on the swings and climbing frames
we crept into the hedge
at the far end of the playground
giggling in delight.
She pulled out her bag
and we shared the bread.

The bell went.
Everyone lined up, and
marched into the class.

'They didn't even notice
We were missing!' she said.
And then someone came out,
calling us.
We sat still, and silent,
eyes dancing and lips twitching.

Soon the whole school walked around
shouting our names,
looking everywhere
but in the hedge.

When we heard a teacher say
'Let's call the police.'
We burst out laughing
'We're not lost, here we are.'
That was my last day
of afternoon activities
at Mackinnon Road Kindergarten.

When I got to P3, we moved to the upper school and could play in a bigger playground, with a climbing frame. We played hopscotch in the space between the head teacher's office and the toilets, just below the windows of the art room. We played 'Mother-may-I' and charades in front of the lower gate. We played marbles wherever we could. In the space between the library and the climbing frame, we skipped with a rope, if someone had brought one. We played 'Keep the kettle boiling, one two three' or 'Not last night, but the night before, 24 robbers came knocking at my door. As I went out to let them in, this is what they said to me …' Or we found a place to do French-skipping with elastic around our legs. The playground was a wonderful place to get dirty, although some children were not able to.

Shirley

I saw her in the playground
that day
from my perch, on top of the
climbing frame.

Her hair held tightly in place.
Her uniform spotless, socks painfully white
walking around like she always did.
But something was different.

Then I noticed
her legs were as stiff
as wooden planks
as she tottered across the playground.
I swung down the climbing frame
careful not to let my panties show
and ran to her, red dust covering
my socks and shoes
hair dishevelled as usual.

'Why are you walking like that?' I asked.
'Because I don't want to crease them.'
'Your legs?' I asked, looking at them again.
'I got them yesterday,' she said,
pointing to her feet sheathed in
a new pair of
dustless, creaseless,
Start-rite shoes.

I opened my mouth,
no words came so
I ran away,
India-rubber legs, swathed
in whitish-brownish socks
stuffed into a pair of

dusty, creased, well-worn
Start-rite shoes.

One of Maama's younger sisters, Aunty Irene, lived in Kololo,
close to us. She was single and would often take us out for treats.
The Wimpy and the drive-in were our favourite outings. Sometimes we would get both – we would stop at Wimpy on our way
to the drive-in. I think it was with her that I ate my first Knicker-
bocker Glory – a layered ice cream fruit dessert in a glass.

Drive-in

She collected us
in her white Mazda
and off to the
drive-in cinema
we went.

There it was
the Big Screen.

Up and down
the terraces
she drove to find
just the right spot.
Car positioned
speakers in place
we watched the movie.

The traffic jammed
as we left.
She cleverly
slipped to the left
onto the pedestrian walk
and we sped along
past the jam
laughing with glee.
Then SPLASH.
Dark greeny spots
all over the car.

'Who farted?' someone asked
as a terrible smell
crept into the car.
To the left of us
below the street light
a sign read: Kampala Sewerage Works.

We had hit a
broken pipe.

Growing up, being chosen to be a bridesmaid at a wedding was
the ultimate. You would get a new dress and new shoes – and
it meant that someone thought you were pretty. Of course this
meant rehearsals before the wedding but they did not always
prepare you for the unexpected.

The Wedding

The flower girls in
pale yellow satin dresses,
white stockings
and blue patent leather shoes,
led the bridal party out of the church.

They stopped outside
the door and waited.

In front of them
two lines of
policemen stood,
blue and gold columns
lining the pathway.

The band began to play …
Suddenly the policemen
made one swift move.
A silver arch formed
over the path,
dazzling bright in the sunlight.

The taller girl froze –
And pulled her cousin back.
The swords
flashed menacingly at them.

'Go on,' smiled the matron,
Gently pushing them forward.

Heart pounding
she grabbed her cousin's hand
and said 'Run!'
They raced through
as if expecting the sword-arch to
come flashing down.

Safe at last
they turned and saw
bride and groom walking
slowly through the silver,
smiling.

Maama and Daddy had a smallholding in Buddo, 12 kilometres out of Kampala. Daddy's grandfather, Micah Sematimba, was a chief in that area and that is where Jajja John grew up, and where my father grew up too. Jajja John had given it to them. Maama had a shamba, a garden where she grew some of our food, on that plot. She varied her crops over the years: matooke, peanuts, beans and maize. Maama went there regularly to pay the workers, to check on her plants and to harvest. She built relationships with people in the community, some of whom were our relatives. I remember visiting a lady who lived close to our smallholding – it might have been Aunty Getu – when I was about eight years old.

Katogo

On the way home
from the farm
Maama stops,
as usual, to pay respects
to the old lady
in the village.

Car parked
on the dusty red road
we walk into
her compound.

Deep red-brown walls
crowned with thatch.
A green forest
of plantains
growing on one side.
Her garden immaculate.

They talk
and I sit on the woven
mukeeka next to them.
She offers me a plate.
'Akatogo ka muwogo n'ebijanjalo,'
she says.

The fragrant aroma

fills my nostrils
and my mouth waters.
Soft beans
in thick sauce
Hints of ghee, coriander and curry
tickle my taste buds.
Muwogo melting
velvety in my mouth.
I savour
each spoonful
oblivious of the two women
next to me.

Then Maama says:
'We must leave now.'
Reluctantly I get up
'Ofumbye nnyo Nyabo,'[6]
I say, as we leave.

Forty odd years later
I do not remember her name
or where her house was,
but the taste
of her katogo
lingers in my mouth.

---

6. Thank you Ma'am for cooking such a tasty meal.

We often had large family gatherings at various homes. My father's mother's family lived in Bulemeezi. They had omu-dalasini (cinnamon trees) growing there and sometimes the bark or leaves were put into tea as it brewed. The memory of the taste lingered, but I did not remember what had been put into the tea, just that it was delicious. Then one day, as I walked home from school, I stopped at a friend's house.

Omudalasini

This afternoon something
drew me to a tree
and I smelt the leaves
Mmmh.

In an instant
I was transported to Ndejje
to Jajja's home
surrounded by trees.

> Someone is boiling tea
> over an open fire.
> She sends us to
> collect leaves,
> from the mudalasini tree.
> She brews them in the tea
> 'Here, drink this my child.'

The fragrance rises
Through my nostrils ...
Mmmh!
I put the cup to my lips,
take a sip.
The flavour
lingers
sweet, spicy, warm ...

Suddenly
I return to the present,
pluck a few leaves
like one grasping at treasure,
take a last deep breath
and
hurry home for tea.

Our house, the last house on our street, had a triangular garden. We shared a fence with two houses at the back – their gates were on the street above ours. Jane and her family lived in one of the houses and we loved playing together. The only problem was that, to visit, we had to walk in the road, all the way round the houses, and our parents did not like us doing that. We didn't like it either, with the lingering fear of soldiers and intelligence men. We did not feel safe.

One day, when we were playing, we made a discovery. The chain-link fence separating their garden from their neighbours, and connecting to our back garden, was incomplete. There was a gap between this fence and the neighbour's. In between, in this gap, was a hedge that came all the way down to our garden. If we hacked away, we could create a passageway, making it possible to move freely between the two houses, without stepping onto the road. So we set to work. For the next few days we would come out after breakfast and work, breaking branches, and begging our gardener to help chop away the hard bits. Eventually we created a pathway. Now we could visit each other at any time and it was easy for our parents to find us. We spent many happy days playing in both gardens – hopscotch, hide-and-seek, climbing trees. We even used the pathway to attend each other's birthday parties.

One afternoon, Jane and I discovered a beehive in the middle of our passageway. The bees were buzzing around quietly. This was a problem. The adults told us we could not use the path until they had got rid of the bees. We waited for them until we realised they were not going to do it immediately; they would do it in their own time. So we helped.

We called Jane's little brothers and sisters and told them to go into the house and not to come out until we called them. Then we found some big sticks. We stood on my side of the passageway and began to hit the hive. All of a sudden a swarm of bees flew out. At that moment we saw Tony, Jane's youngest brother, running towards us, through the bees. Jane ran and grabbed him. He was screaming. We started running towards our house shouting 'BEES!'

My cousin Kitongo was sitting in front of the house with Fay and Chris. When he heard us, he picked them up, one by one, and took them into the house and locked the door. We had to run round to the other side of the house. When we got inside, Tony was screaming, tears rolling down a hive of swellings on his face. Jane had a couple of stings and I had escaped without any. When things calmed down, Jane and I got a long, serious talking to.

The next morning we found the bees had made a new hive, in a tree overhanging our driveway. The fire brigade was called to come and get rid of them. Later that day Kamoti, our gardener, explained to us that normally they wait until evening and then they smoke the bees away, because in the evening bees are calmer. And we were told how dangerous bee stings could be.

3 *Snuffing out the fire*

But one harsh winter, a dark enchantment befell the tribe. The breath of an evil spirit blew in an icy gale across the land snuffing out the council fires, shredding the delicate webs of stories that bound mothers to daughters, fathers to sons, neighbours to neighbours.
ANNE CUSHMAN

After the coup in 1971, things changed in Uganda. Amin started killing soldiers of Langi and Acholi heritage. He suspected they were loyal to Obote, the president he had ousted. For the civilian population, life went on as normal. We were not aware that things were changing rapidly, and for the children, life was the same.

Then, in March 1972, Amin broke all ties with the Israelis and they were expelled from Uganda. In August, he announced that all Indians, Goans and Pakistanis had 90 days to leave the country. I remember the television announcements and the daily reminder of how many more days they had left. I remember overhearing conversations amongst the adults, wondering how the families would manage. We learnt of Indians who had committed suicide by gassing themselves in their garages. They weren't allowed to leave with any money or gold. There were stories of them hiding their jewellery.

One evening, driving through Kampala with Daddy, we saw lots and lots of families of Indians outside the Parliament buildings. I don't know whether it was a demonstration, or whether they had nowhere to go. I looked at their faces through the window. There was an embankment of stone with some men and children standing on it. Some were wearing punjabis, the ballooned pants, with long shirts and Nehru collars. There were women in saris, or the pantsuits they wore, with scarves around their necks, and the red spots on their foreheads. The children were playing. The women and men huddled together in conversation. Some young men stared at us, their eyes hard to read. As we passed, another car drove by and someone shouted, 'Sixty more days!' or something like that. My father shook his head.

One of his Indian friends, I think it was Babu, brought his statues of his gods and asked my parents to keep them for him. For a long time they were in our sitting room on the display shelf, a small act of defiance by my parents, I think. We had Indian and Goan friends at school who slowly disappeared – Nigel D'Souza, Shanaz Patel, Palavi Patel – and we never heard about them again.

The expulsion of the Indians also impacted on the Ugandan nationals. I remember watching Amin on TV, walking down one of the streets and handing over shops to people who were simply walking on the streets. The adults shook their heads and said he was crazy. Some of those who were given businesses ran them well, others learnt how to run them, and some ran them into the ground. Goods became scarce, and factories limped on as people became more competent in managing them. Imported goods in the port of Mombasa went unclaimed, to the benefit of Kenyan businesses. And as the Ugandans staggered, the Kenyans found a market in Uganda and began a brisk export business. We lined up for sugar, milk, cooking oil, soap, salt. Many times, whole families lined up because if there was sugar, one could only buy one or two kilogrammes. People started buying in bulk when they could and many began to hoard, sharing only with family members. Sometimes Maama would get a 25-kilogramme bag of sugar and then we would measure out some for aunties and uncles, as well as our grandparents and the staff at home. All the supplies were kept under lock and key and rations dished out on a daily basis. When Maama was not there, I kept the key.

One afternoon in September 1972, while we were at school, the bell rang and we were all ushered into the hall with our bags. This was strange, as we normally had assembly in the morning and we never came to the hall with our bags. We were told that Tanzanian soldiers and Ugandan 'rebels' were coming to Kampala to fight and that we had to wait there for our parents to fetch us. They were said to be about a hundred kilometres from Kampala. Some of us normally walked home after school and this presented us with a problem.

I saw one girl crying, asking the teachers how her parents would find her. The adults' grim faces scared us. I can't remember who fetched me. When I got home, I remember Walukuwa, our houseman, in a panic, closing all the windows, while I, in my desire to keep things normal, kept opening them and singing. I did not want to be afraid, but I was. We switched on the radio, listening for what was happening and waiting for Maama and Daddy to come back home.

Maama was at the university working on her master's research thesis. She came home much later. She had been in the library, in the area reserved for master's and doctoral students. They each had cubicles that were soundproof, and she was in there transcribing tapes she had collected in the field, for her research on the oral literature of the Bamasaba, her people.

One of her lecturers had come past that afternoon and knocked on the door of the cubicle next to her, calling out to another colleague. She had seen them having an earnest conversation and thought nothing of it. Her colleague went back into the cubicle, packed up his things and left. Maama continued to work for a few more hours. When she packed up, she walked into an empty library: not a soul in sight, the lights off and the doors locked. In the meantime Daddy was trying to find her. She managed to open one of the side doors and leave, meeting Daddy somewhere on the campus.

That was the first of many attempted coups by Ugandans in exile in Tanzania and other parts of the world, and it failed. The aftermath of that was the abduction and killing of many of Uganda's brilliant academic, business and community-building citizens: Ben Kiwanuka, the chief justice; Frank Kalimuzo, the vice-chancellor of Makerere University; Joseph Mubiru, the governor of the Bank of Uganda; Basil Bataringaya, the first leader of the opposition in the Ugandan parliament and minister of internal affairs, and later his wife; James Bwogi, a well-loved TV personality; William Kalema, minister of commerce from 1967 to 1971; the list goes on.

From 1972 onwards, the term 'Gundi bamututte' or 'Gundi baamututte' became part of our speech: 'So and so has been taken' or 'So and so was taken.' People were taken from their offices, their homes or as they dropped their children at school. Sometimes they were pulled or pushed into a car, sometimes shoved into the boot. Some were never, ever seen again. If your person came back, or their body was found, you were considered lucky.

As children, we overheard adults speaking. We all knew someone who had had someone taken. Then rumours circulated that the State Research Bureau threw bodies away in the forest at Namanve and Mabira. The villagers there knew what time they would come. People who had lost a family member or friend would go to the forest, sometimes daily, to see if they could find their loved ones, sifting through bodies sometimes whole, sometimes beheaded. There are families who did this for months and never found their loved ones.

Those who came back were changed. Some found words to speak about what had happened. Others never spoke about it again.

It was also around this time that men who had been arrested as part of the attempted coup were shot in a firing squad at the eSaawa ya Queen – the Queen's Clock Tower on Entebbe Road. They were tied up, with a hood over their heads, and shot in front of a crowd and TV cameras. Our parents tried to shield us from this but it was on the news, in the newspapers, on the street, at school.

One morning we woke up and next to our gate, underneath

the mango tree that overhung our fence, was a car burnt to cinders. My parents had heard a single gunshot the night before and when they peered through the curtains, they saw the car burning. No one dared to go out to see what was happening. At breakfast I heard my mother tell my father: 'You must go and look at the car. It happened outside our home. It is terrible and if people don't see you, they might think you were involved.' He went, albeit reluctantly. I think there was always the fear that it might be someone you knew or some Intelligence man might falsely arrest you because you are on the scene. We weren't allowed to go and look.

The taking and killing of people lead to another trend: people leaving the country. Sometimes it was planned and sometimes it was quick. Families were split apart. I found it distressing – one day someone was at school and then they too disappeared. At first I would think that they might be sick. Like when my cousins, the Bigirwenkyas, left. Hosea was in the same class as me and we were both going to be part of the end of year concert. We were acting out a poem with five other children. There was a narrator, three 'Ladies' and three 'Dukes': Florence, Patricia, I think, and I were the Ladies, and Hosea, Harold and I think it was Johnny, were the Dukes.

Somewhere in the midst of the rehearsals, Hosea stopped coming to school. Someone else took his place in the concert. Months later, I learnt that they were in the States and I had inherited their piano; the only good thing about their leaving. Estella and I could no longer walk up Muwafu Road and meet Norah and Hosea at the big muwafu tree on Akii Bua Road and then walk to their house.

I only learnt the truth recently. Uncle Big had been

appointed a minister in Amin's first cabinet, and when Amin started killing off his ministers and senior government officials, Uncle was warned that he was on the hit list. So he left, quietly, and the family followed soon after. That was the general pattern. People, often men, would be warned that they were on the list. If they were lucky, they would escape and their families would follow later. There were many who were warned but refused to leave. Or maybe they did not believe it would happen.

A couple of years after the Bigs left Kampala, at the beginning of P6, I waited for Maggi, my best friend, to come back to school. After a week she had still not come back and no one could tell me what had happened.

In 1973 Idi Amin started pushing his Muslim faith more overtly. He banned women from wearing miniskirts, wigs and trousers, claiming it was indecent. The ban on trousers was soon rescinded but miniskirts and wigs became a no-no. Women walking around in town would be arrested for wearing skirts that ended just above their knees.

Our mothers, and indeed, Ugandan women in general, were fashion-conscious and they dressed well. They wore short dresses and stylish wigs. We began to hear that people were made to eat their wigs. True or not, the way women dressed changed. Short dresses became a thing of the past and maxis and midis, the dresses that stopped on your calf, became the order of the day.

When I was about 11, I was terrified that I would be arrested. I went to school to get an identity card so that they would know I was underage, even though my mother assured me that nothing would happen. I did not want to take a chance. People started changing their faith to Islam in order to 'be safe'. By

1978, Amin had made Friday a day of rest, so the working week was effectively only four days. People were supposed to rest on Friday, as it was the Muslim holy day, go to work and school on Saturday, and then rest on Sunday. But some people just made the weekend three days long.

Roadblocks also became common. Soldiers manned them and they could make you sit there for as long as they wanted. I remember the roadblock on the road from Kampala to Masaka, as we crossed over the Mayanja River wetlands, on the way to Buddo. One Saturday morning I went with my parents to Buddo, to their smallholding. I loved singing in the car, as loudly as I could, but as we approached the roadblock my singing stopped. We were told to get out of the car and stood there for about 30 minutes. Then they let us go. Of course I wanted to go back home immediately, but my parents said no. They did not want to let the thugs win. This is what Uganda had mutated into.

For many, the horror of what happened in those times could not be put into words. Some did not talk about it for years; others remain silent. Some vowed to fight this evil, either from within or from outside. Some did whatever they could just to survive and to keep their families alive in Uganda. Some left and tried to forget, tried to shut away all that had happened. Sometimes they even changed their names. But Uganda lived on inside them.

One afternoon I was at home with Fay and Chris; my cousin Joyce, who was then about 19; Walukuwa, who did the house-work; and Milicah and Grace, the young women who helped with Fay and Chris. My father was away on a business trip and my two elder sisters were at boarding school. My mother went, with the driver, Muleefu, to our smallholding in Buddo to get plantains and cassava, and to pay the workers. By dusk they were not back. The sun slid behind the hills and the sky turned an inky black and still Maama and Muleefu had not returned. There was an unofficial curfew in Kampala and everyone tried to be home before dark.

Where were they? Unpredictable soldiers manned the roadblock at the Mayanja River swamps. What if they were in a bad mood? I had heard somebody speaking in hushed tones of bodies being thrown into the swamp.

As the darkness deepened, the adults in the house started saying: 'What if the soldiers have taken her?' 'They might even have killed them.' 'What will we do if she does not come home?' 'I don't think they are coming back.' My heart sounded like a drum in my ears. I could not breathe. I prayed silently that Maama was alright and that she would come home. I looked at Fay and Chris, who could understand but could not talk, and tried to change the subject so that they would not be scared, all the while imploring God to bring my mother home.

After what seemed like a lifetime we heard the engine of a car in the driveway. When I saw Maama coming out of the car I ran and held her tight, sobs racking my body. They were safe. Maama held me, asking, 'Philippa, kyi kyi? What is wrong?' When I calmed down, I asked her why they were so late. I told her we thought the soldiers had taken them. They'd had a puncture and did not have a jack so they had to wait for help. There was no way they could contact us.

I can only imagine what Maama and Muleefu must have been thinking and feeling as they drove back to Kampala in the dark. Every sound, every strange car following them, would have made their hearts beat a little faster, the hair on the backs of their necks stand up. Every kilometre closer to home would have brought a small sense of relief.

One of the things I did was take care of Fay and Chris, even if I did not have to. I helped feed and dress them, as well as trying to understand what they were saying. I liked bathing with Chris because I could carry him. We would play in the water for a long time, until our fingers were old and shrivelled like prunes. One day, as we were bathing Chris, his eyes froze, his body stiffened and I knew the attack would come in seconds. This happened often and I knew that I needed to lie him down and clear his tongue. But we were in a bath.

I held him with one hand, pulled out the plug with the other and shouted for help. I am not sure how long the convulsion lasted but it felt like forever. Did someone come to help, or did I manage to get him out of the bath? We put Chris onto his bed – everyone except Maama. I went downstairs and found her standing in the dining room. Standing still, with one hand on the back of a chair. I asked her why she had not come up. She replied that she was coming, and she did.

As a child I could not understand. I had expected her to come up and say well done. Now, as a mother, I stand in her shoes and feel what she might have been thinking and feeling. Chris could have drowned in the bath, with me trying to help him. The dread of what might have been and relief that we were okay, washed over her, holding her frozen at the chair, as she breathed a silent prayer of thanks, and of 'Why us, Lord?', of 'No more, please.'

Our parents did their best to keep the horror of the regime away from us, but even parents have their limitations.

Velvet Skies

11 years old
and afraid we have lost
my father
forever.

Three days ago
he was taken
from his office
to Naguru.

Nsubuga came home
driving like a maniac.
He told Maama.

Now the house is full of people
that we keep serving tea.
Are they mourning him?
Are they praying?
Are they planning ways
to bring him back?

My heart is heavy.
Many others have been taken

and never returned.

I retreat to the only place
I can be alone –
the bathroom.

As I run the bath
I remember Maama saying calmly,
on the first day,
'Your father has been taken,
but don't worry, we will be alright.'
I believe her.

She was later allowed to visit him.
And when she returned she said,
'Your father said he loves you.
No matter what happens you must
walk tall, with your head held up high.
He has done nothing wrong.'

Tears roll down my face,
the comforting warmth of water
enfolds me.
I stare at the velvety skies
through the frosted glass window –
Light blue ... deeper blue ... purply blue ...
It is dusk.
God made this time specially.

'God,' I speak

in our special time alone.
'Let Daddy come home today.'
I am praying for all of us –
Maama, Maliza, Estella,
Fay, Chris and me.

Finished, I look up.
The sky is now black
and my fingers old and wrinkled.
I slip on my pyjamas.
Walking down the stairs
headlights sweep into the driveway.

I hear the pounding in my chest
as I peer through the French windows.
A white Datsun with UVS number plates
stops in front of the house.
The car doors open
and out he steps –
'DADDY!' I scream
and start to let him in.
Behind him a dark man follows.

'Ssh,' say the adults,
as they push me away.
I do not know their fear –
many have been returned
only to be taken again
or killed at the door.

'Daddy,' I say,
squeezing past them
hugging him.
We are wrapped in velvety skies.

The man in the shadows looks on:
'You are happy to see your daddy?'
he asks.

Silently
we walk into the house
and lock the doors.
Daddy is back.
Black turns back to velvet.

One afternoon, soon after Daddy had come out of prison, the telephone rang. The man on the other end asked if Mr Barlow was in. Daddy was there, so I said, 'Yes, would you like to speak to him?'

He said, 'No, it's okay.' I asked who was speaking and he said, 'Mr Bob.'

I thought nothing of it and did not tell Daddy that a 'Mr Bob' had called. A little while later a cream UVS vehicle drove into our yard and out popped an old white man looking for Daddy. By this time, he had gone out; I hadn't seen him go. Maama was in Mbale doing her research. Maliza and I answered the door. When we told Bob that Dad was out, he said, 'Well, I telephoned earlier and I was told that he was here.'

'Oh, was it you?' I said. 'I didn't tell him that you called.'

'Are you sure he is out?' he demanded.

My sister Maliza, tall, with a big afro, looked directly at him and said, 'Yes we are. Do you think we are lying? Do you want to search the house?' He backed down then and went away. As the car disappeared out the gate I felt a cold shiver run down my spine. I also felt a burst of pride at my big sister.

An hour later, Uncle Gus, our neighbour, called and asked me what had happened. He said Mr Bob had gone to their house first, thinking it was ours. I found out later that 'Mr Bob' was Bob Astles, the greatly feared Englishman who was involved with the secret police or Intelligence. That evening Daddy had to take Maliza and her friend Jennifer back to Gayaza High School. Fay, Chris and I were going too. Uncle Gus looked at Daddy and said, 'Henry, I am coming with you. I was in the army: if they want to do anything, they will have to go through me!' He would not take no for an answer. So we all squeezed into the car and drove to Gayaza and back. In those days you did not always have neighbours who would stand by you like that. We were growing suspicious of each other because of the regime. I will always be grateful for our neighbours, and especially for Uncle Gus.

In 1975 Amin was made the Chairman of the Organisation of African Unity (OAU) and so Uganda hosted the OAU Summit that year. It was exciting – even with the darkness happening in the country. There were new cars bought for each of the heads of state and their entourages, each with special number plates. We learnt the names of all the countries, their capital cities and their presidents, such as President Mobutu Sese Seko Kuku Ngbendu Wa Za Banga of Zaire and President Omar Bongo of Gabon. We learnt that Ouagadougou, pronounced 'Wagadugu', was the capital of Upper Volta – now Burkina Faso – and we could recognise all their flags too.

As part of the conference, it was announced that there would be gymnastics displays at the Nakivubo Stadium, with the secondary schools doing the gymnastics and primary schools creating a visual background display. My school was chosen to be part of the visual display. We went to the stadium every day during our holidays to learn what to do. It was daunting because there were always so many people at the stadium. There were hundreds of primary school children, hundreds of high school children and then there were army recruits who were called Rikurutus or Kurutus. Those were the ones who scared me the most. We sat in the sun all day long, and at lunchtime huddled together with our schoolmates and ate our packed lunch. In the background, at lunchtime, Lingala music played over the speakers. If it rained, we stood under the stands.

The instructors were Korean. We sat in the stands, each of us holding an A3 book with many pages. Each one of us had our specially assigned position and book. Opposite us, on the other side of the stadium, was our conductor. A number would be displayed, a signal made, and we would have to turn to that page in our books, in unison. The result would be a big picture, a backdrop to what the high school students were doing.

While we did our bit, the high school students practised formations on the field in front of us in time with the music that blared out of the speakers. In the beginning, it was hard to focus on the numbers and turn our pages on time because the formations in front of us were so amazing to see. But after lots of practice, we got it.

There were also a group of other students who did a march past, as did the army recruits. The recruits held large, rifle-length sticks as they marched. One day there was an altercation between some of the recruits and some high school boys. All of a sudden the recruits were chasing the boys, beating them up with their big sticks. The boys responded by hurling soft-drink bottles that they found in cases nearby. We ran under the stands and prayed. We watched as the recruits beat a boy up so badly he could have died. Finally, someone managed to calm the situation down.

From that point on, we did not dare even look at the recruits. We found ways of walking around the stadium, taking long routes if necessary, to avoid them. I told my parents about it that evening and they said that maybe I should stay home. But I did not stop going to the stadium because rumour had it that we would be expelled from school if we did not attend the gymnastics. Nothing my parents said made me stop going, even though I was terrified. I did not want to be expelled.

My parents had a house in Muyenga, or Tank Hill as it was called, because there was a big water reservoir at the top of the hill. The December after Daddy's arrest, they planned for us to spend Christmas there, since there were no tenants in the house and it would be a change. Piece by piece, furniture and crockery were moved to the house, and one evening, I think it was Christmas Eve, we moved to Muyenga. We shared a lovely Christmas and never moved back to number 1A Kafu Road. This was the beginning of a much bigger move.

I made friends with Silas and Paul, who lived up the road, and Charlie, who lived across the road. We rode bicycles up and down the hill every day. I even learnt to ride without holding my handlebars. I had cropped hair then and was often in shorts or trousers, and I was always with the boys. Once, riding past some ladies, I heard them debate my gender.

'You see that one, she is a girl.'

'No, it's a boy. What girl would ride a bicycle like that?'

I was surprised and tickled, but it was true: it was not common to see girls riding bicycles, wearing pants or climbing trees the way I loved to.

We settled in Muyenga comfortably. It was not built up then and we could walk across the hill to Kansanga, using many different footpaths, to visit the Mukasas and other friends. Today, not a single one of those paths remains. Charlie and I had a special bond. His house was opposite ours and we spent many evenings sitting under the tree near our gate, or standing at the gate talking. One day, his father disappeared, and a few days later we heard that he had been killed. Soon after, they moved away, and we saw each other only once or twice more.

The year we moved to Muyenga was my last year in primary school and so I had to study for my Primary Leaving Exams (PLE), which I hated. It was fashionable, during term time, to go to teachers' homes for tuition, and that's how they supplemented their meagre salaries. I was signed up for extra maths and geography with our teacher Mr Ruhumuriza. Two or three times a week a group of us walked from school to William Street, at the bottom of town, for our lessons. That street was known as 'teacher street,' as many teachers lived in the flats there. Children came from various rival primary schools – Kitante, Norman Godino, Shimoni and, of course, our school,

Nakasero – so there were always fights or bragging sessions. The popular kids tended to hang out together but I never quite made it into that group; I was on the margins.

The walk to William Street was both fun and scary. There was a big group of us who walked out of the top gate of the school towards All Saints Cathedral. As we passed Kampala Kindergarten, next to our school and opposite the French Embassy, we got ready to run. Next to the embassy was a big concrete building with solid walls around it – the dreaded National State Research Bureau. The gates were manned by the special police force, whose uniform was different from the other policemen. We all knew that it belonged to the secret police and had heard that people who went there never came out alive. What if they caught us and pulled us into the building? We only stopped running when we got to the church, a block away.

I hated the lessons. I felt awkward and did not fit in with the other kids. I hated the feeling I had every time I walked past the State Research building. And we always did the subject that the teacher had prepared for the day, regardless of whether it was what you needed extra support in. It was like being in class all over again. Luckily I did not go to teacher street for long. The petrol crisis arrived, classes were suspended and I never went back.

Maama devised another plan. She got me past papers and on Saturdays and during the holidays I had to complete one exam paper a day in the set time and only after I had done that would she let me go and play. It worked.

In 1976 Amin declared that he was claiming back the part of Kenya that had originally been part of Uganda before the scramble for Africa changed everything. There was a big fight between the two governments. Then some Palestinians, and some Germans who supported them, hijacked an Air France plane with many Israelis on it and brought it to Uganda. They were demanding that Israel free a number of Palestinian political prisoners. Many countries refused to support the hijackers, but Amin supported them. The hostages were held in a building at the old airport that was used by the air force. Kenya joined in, supporting the Israeli government in their negotiations with the hijackers and Amin.

Our parents were once again listening to the BBC and Radio Uganda for news, and we would share the little information we had at school. Then, one day, the Israeli's flew in, freed the hostages, killed many Ugandan soldiers, and burnt our MiG aircraft. Amin chased a number of Kenyans from the country and the tensions returned.

The Kenyan government closed the border and our imports, especially fuel and paraffin, were stuck there. The petrol reserves began to dwindle and people lined up for hours for the little petrol that trickled through. Uganda is a landlocked country and our fuel supply and almost all our imports came through Kenya. Nsubuga, Daddy's driver, would turn off the ignition and let the car kuwondowa down hills on its own momentum in order to preserve fuel. We started taking a packed lunch or buying lunch at school. The Onabas, who lived near to the school, were close family friends. My parents arranged that Daddy and I would eat lunch there, so on school days at lunchtime I walked to their house. After school I walked to Daddy's office at Farmer's House, where the Lint Marketing Board was based, and then we drove home.

One afternoon I arrived at the office and Daddy said, 'Nsubuga did not get any petrol today. We have to walk home.' So I picked up my school bag, and Dad his briefcase, and we started walking, joining a long line of people who were also walking home.

As we got to the railway crossing near Kibuli, a kind gentleman stopped his car and said, 'Mr Barlow, you cannot walk: we will give you a lift.' I have no idea who this person was but I will never forget his kindness.

The car was already full so Daddy said, with a smile, 'Thank you, but it's okay. We will pass through Kisugu. It won't be a long walk.' The gentleman insisted and even asked one person to get out. Embarrassed, Daddy thanked him and we squeezed into the car. I was relieved because it was a long way to walk. They dropped us at the top of the hill, close to home, and drove away.

Times like these seem to bring out the best or the worst in people. It was the kindness and generosity of people like this, sometimes strangers, which kept us going through those difficult times.

When we were in P7, a new boy, Noha, joined our class. He was said to be the son of one of Amin's ministers who was greatly feared. Noha was much bigger than most of us. He was older than we were and he was his father's son, so all the stories we had heard about his father we projected onto him. Soldiers drove him to school and this made him more frightening. It did not help that he was bad-tempered too.

One day we were sitting in our classroom, built to house 25 children, but with close to 40 now. Mr Ruhumuriza had gone to the office for something, leaving us to finish some work. Noha was next to Merida. She said something that annoyed him. As he stood up, all of us sitting close to them jumped out of our seats, over chairs and desks and huddled against the classroom walls. We stood there staring at Noha and Merida, breath held. Noha stopped, looked at us with a slight frown on his face and said, 'I am not going to beat her.' We slowly went back to our seats. That was the first time he became aware of how afraid of him we were and we saw a touch of humanity in him. From that day, something changed and we were not as afraid of him as before.

A loud scream broke through my dream early one morning. It was Estella. She woke up and opened her curtains to a skull in the middle of the garden, grinning at her. We all rushed to her room and looked out of her window. Maguja, our dog, was running in circles, close to the skull, barking, but she never touched it.

The day before, someone had brought the stump of a banana tree, a kitooke, and laid it in our neighbour's driveway. They had laid a skull, a human skull, on the kitooke with a note. There was talk that this was an act of witchcraft because one of the neighbour's sons had broken someone's heart. No one, it seems, had seen who had put it there and people were afraid to move it. We had no idea how it got into our garden but we suspected that they had thrown it over.

My mother was clear about her beliefs. She said, 'I do not believe in this witchcraft. I don't know if someone is trying to scare me, but they will *not* scare me or my children.' She asked for a cardboard box and a stick. Then she went into the garden, rolled the skull into the box, carried it to the gate and put it down next to the dustbin. She made a speech to all the people in the neighbourhood who were staring at her in dismay about not being afraid, about knowing we were protected by God. Then we went about our day as usual. I think she might even have called the police, but they did not come. The skull stayed there all day.

In the late afternoon, a group of teenage girls came, picked up the box and left.

4 Smouldering embers

What makes the desert beautiful is that somewhere it hides a well.
ANTOINE DE SAINT-EXUPÉRY

Aunty Violet

She was a tall, dark
voluptuous woman
with eyes that spoke more
than her mouth did.

Waiting outside his office
she sat still and upright
hands folded in her lap.

Only her eyes hinted
at the fire within.

Finally they let her in.
Mr Bob sat across the desk
his face pink and sweaty
on this humid afternoon.
'Where is my husband?'
she asked quietly.
Her eyes glinting.
Her body still.
'I don't know,' he replied.

Slowly she leaned forward
and said,
'You have taken him
again
and I have come to fetch him.'

'I do not know your husband.'
His thin pale lips
twitched as he spoke,
his eyes, cold and empty,
staring back into hers.

Suddenly
she stood
and pushed his desk up
against his big belly
pinning him helpless

against the wall.

Her eyes blazing,
she said,
'Bobu!
My husband has done nothing wrong
and I will NOT leave here without him!
I will NOT raise my children alone.
WHERE IS MY HUSBAND?'

Mr Bob's eyes opened wide
and he gasped.
Face ashen,
pinned between wall and desk
unable to move or breathe,
he looked into her burning eyes
her tall body towering over him
and
suddenly he remembered
her husband ... and
where he was.

'Please Madam,
let go of the desk,'
he wheezed.
'Your husband will
be here soon.'

That day

her husband came back home
never to be taken again.

At some point after our move to Muyenga, Daddy resigned from his position as managing director of the Lint Marketing Board. The government accepted his decision. It was announced on national television, as part of the 8pm news. I remember Maama and Daddy dancing around the sitting room, laughing. I joined in, unsure what was going on, but happy to see them so happy.

We threw a big party at home to celebrate his resignation. So many of their old friends and all the family were there. Then one day Daddy brought us papers to apply for passports. I thought nothing much of it. My greatest worry was that I did not have a signature and did not know how I would get one. I was told not to worry; I could use my initials and surname, so my signature became 'PAN Barlow.' I was proud of it.

Later that year, Dad left for Addis Ababa, Ethiopia, to become the first secretary general of the African Association for Public Administration and Management (AAPAM), which had its headquarters in the UN Economic Commission for Africa building in Addis. We remained in Uganda, waiting.

We never really spoke about how he left but I was aware that he did not want to leave as a refugee and he had found a way to do that, probably because he was not a politician. He came home that Christmas and then went back with Maama. I remember that because, before he arrived home, there were many hushed conversations between the adults. I overheard someone saying, 'Maybe he should stay in Nairobi.' I think they suspected that he would be arrested, or worse. We were lucky there was no incident. He left with Maama soon after Christmas and they were not around for my confirmation. My godparents – Aunty Winnie, Aunty Ida and Uncle Dennis – stood in for them and created a wonderful celebration. When Maama returned a few weeks later, life went on as usual, but without Daddy. She brought me a dark brown cross made of plaited leather. I treasured it.

Thirty years later, twelve days after Daddy died, on the day that would have been their fiftieth wedding anniversary, we had a small gathering at home to celebrate their life together. Mr Nagaga, a family friend who had been in Addis with Daddy spoke about the delicate negotiations that had taken place to enable Daddy to work in Addis. There is a lot about those days that I do not know.

Maama always had compassion for the underdog, be it a human being or an animal. After Daddy left, she found Simba, a mongrel that had been tormented by the children in the neighbourhood. She had wandered into our garden through the gate and hid near the staff quarters. She was a small dog with a short-haired toffee-brown coat. Her big eyes changed through various shades of brown, depending on her mood. When anyone except Maama approached, her tail curled between her legs and she growled and bared her teeth. We all wanted to get rid of her but Maama refused.

She fed her, spoke to her gently and slowly started stroking her. Maama named her Simba. She always said dogs' names should start with an S because she said they heard it better. After a few days, Simba started to relax and slowly warm to us. She began to put on weight and started wagging her tail when we approached her. Those big eyes that were full of fear warmed up and became like pools of honey. We grew to love Simba in the same way that Maama did.

Simba became one of the many dogs we had, maybe one too many, so when Uncle Dennis said he was looking for a dog, Maama gave him Simba. We were sad to see her go, but Uncle Dennis's house was within walking distance so we could visit her.

One day Uncle Dennis came to our house at around lunchtime to fetch Maama. They were going to a funeral. He mentioned that he thought he had run over Simba as he left home. She had yelped, stood up and run into the hedge. He did not check on her because he was late, and she had stood up. I started to argue with him but they were late and he left with Maama. I immediately walked up the road to my friends Silas and Paul and asked them to come with me.

We hurried up the red murram road to Uncle's house, feeling the gravel crunch under our feet. Uncle Dennis, like many people in those days, had a padlock on the gate. When visitors came, they hooted and someone came to open the gate. It was a security measure to guard against kondos who came wielding pangas, and the police and army, who were also thugs. We were on foot, so the house help did not open the gate for us because they did not see or hear us. In the end we climbed over the gate and went to the house and asked them if Simba was okay. They did not know, so we began to look for her.

We found her under the hedge, whimpering. We slowly coaxed her out and found that she had broken her leg. We gave her milk and then took her home to 'treat' her. She was too heavy for us to carry so we borrowed a wheelbarrow from Silas and Paul's house, lined it with hessian sacks so she would be comfortable, and wheeled her to our house. We laid her on a table in the garage, found something we could use as splints and cloth we could use as a bandage, and tied up her leg. Then we gave her milk again and decided unanimously that Uncle Dennis did not deserve Simba and that we were going to relieve him of the animal.

Hours later Uncle Dennis brought Maama back and we told them what we had done and that we had decided Uncle Dennis was not a fit dog owner. Maama listened to us patiently, and then said, 'The dog is your Uncle's. He had an accident that he thought was not serious. Thank you for taking care of Simba.' So Uncle went home with the dog. I did not say goodbye.

There were no further incidents with Simba. What we as children had read as negligence was an honest assumption that the dog was okay.

First day

Maama took me to Gayaza
on that first day
a coming of age
I could hardly wait for.

That afternoon, with
suitcase packed
metal tuckbox cradling
roasted peanuts, home-baked
cookies, sugar, margarine
I jumped in and

the car refused to start.
Daddy away in Addis Ababa,
Uncle Dennis and
Uncle Patrick still at work.
I held back the tears.

It was the first day.

As the sun began to set
the car miraculously started.
'Why don't we go tomorrow?'
she asked.
'I really want to go today.'

We packed the car again.
Torch in the glove box and
Uncle Patrick next to Maama
in case the car broke down.

It was almost dark when we arrived
the dorms lit up and a-buzz.

I was there on the first day.

And she returned home
under the warm dark
blanket of the night.

Weeks later
Estella told me.

On their way home,
as they rounded the corner
from Kibuli to Kisugu,
her headlights shone
on a pick-up truck parked by the roadside.
Then like spotlights on soldiers
urinating by the roadside.

She dimmed them immediately.

'Simama!' they shouted,
'Stop!'
Pulling her out of the car
with a slap.

'How dare you shine lights on us
as we help ourselves!'

They grabbed the torch
shoved Maama and Uncle
back in the car, shouting,
'Drive! And if we find you again
only God knows what will happen!'

She drove like a madwoman
on that dusty road
past the church and
as they got to the tarred road
a pick-up truck appeared.

'It's okay,' said Uncle
'It's not the same car.'

Home safe and sound,
but only just.
And never said a word
to spoil my first day.

Gayaza High School was rich in traditions grounded in its missionary heritage. It was an all-girls' boarding school that aimed to develop the students more than just academically. There was a strong programme to develop us into accomplished women. When we arrived in Senior 1, the first year of secondary school, we went to class in our own clothes and were handed a couple of incomplete school uniforms. We were taught, in the home economics class, how to embroider the school badge and sew it onto our dress, then how to sew the buttonholes, sew on buttons and hem the dress. We were given a week to finish sewing our two or three uniforms. As soon as you finished sewing your uniform, you could wear it. Sewing the badge was the hardest thing to do. Each morning I woke up and realised that there were fewer and fewer of us who had not finished sewing our uniforms. I finally asked someone to help me with the badges.

We were also taught how to starch our belts so they would not fold when we sat. The dresses were a simple design that would have looked like sacks if it weren't for the starched belt around the waist and the different colours: dark blue, yellow, green, pink, powder blue, maroon.

I was in Sherborne House, the house all my family had stayed in. It was one of the oldest houses in the school and the ablutions block was archaic. Estella was in Mary Stuart, the senior block for Sherborne. We were each given a metal bucket with our name on it. Come bath time, we went into the bathroom, which was one large room with taps along the wall. You filled your bucket with cold water, found a space where you would not get into someone's way, and took a bath. If you were lucky to have a kettle or heating stick, you could enjoy a warm bath, but the bath was in the public space. After a while, we all got used to it. No one noticed what the next person was doing or looked like.

By the time I got to Gayaza, life in Uganda was tough – there were all sorts of shortages. Breakfast was sometimes a cup of black tea and a handful of roasted soya beans – or a mug of posho (maize meal) porridge. The kitchen staff would add only a pinch of sugar, so it was good to have your own. Lunch and supper were often posho and beans.

I was lucky on two counts, though. Firstly, Uncle Hugo, Daddy's brother, and Aunty Ntongo lived on the university farm next to the school. Every evening Estella and I would walk to the gate to collect a bottle of milk each. That was a great luxury and lifesaver. We were not allowed to go over to their house but once or twice we snuck over. There was no permanent guard at that gate. Secondly, Estella was in S6 and she had privileges that I could sometimes take advantage of. If I desperately needed boiled water to make tea or bushera – millet porridge, a staple in many boarding schools in Uganda at the time – I would go up to her and get some. We would often make this after evening prep, or on the weekend, to supplement our meagre meals. Estella could ask me for extra sugar when she needed it, so it worked for both of us.

The dining hall was not big enough to hold all the girls so the meals were in two shifts. The shifts were according to houses – half came in the first shift and the other half in the second. Each house in each shift had a turn to wash the plates and make the dining room ready for the next group or the next meal. One lunchtime we were served posho with grated boiled egg sprinkled over it, and a watery, grey groundnut sauce. I was appalled. I did not know how I was going to eat it. Then I looked up and saw Estella and her friends leave the dining room, so I followed. I knew that they were going to cook – we were in the first lunch shift, so there was enough time. They tried to send me back telling me that I was breaking the rules, but I refused, so they let me tag along. We went to one of the other houses, Kennedy or Corby. Someone had rice and other food, so they cooked for us, using utensils that they were not supposed to have at school. I made the most of having a big sister in the school.

We were allowed to plait our hair as long as we combed it out on Friday and only re-plaited it on Sunday after chapel. There were girls in the school who were good at plaiting hair and if you were lucky, they would do it for you. Or you learnt quickly how to plait it for yourself.

Roll call, which happened at least once a day in the evening, and twice on Sundays, was announced by the drumming of a specific rhythm outside chapel. There were senior girls who were assigned this duty. When you heard the drums saying, 'Damali nkusigudde, Damali nkusigudde,' you knew it was roll call.

Every morning at 6.15am, each girl reported for housework duty in some part of the school, finished this in 30 minutes, returned to their dormitory, dressed and reported for breakfast at 7.15am. Housework ranged from cleaning the dormitories, classrooms, the chapel or the staffroom, to smoking the pit-latrines, peeling matooke or potatoes for lunch, or working in the headmistress's house. Classes that took agriculture as a subject (which meant all S1s) had a week when they went to the school farm instead of doing housework. Each class had at least one early morning PE lesson with Miss Cutler. This often meant that we were out on the lawns doing Scottish country dancing, which was taught in many schools in Uganda.

Pocket money was paid in with school fees, even though most parents slipped their daughters something extra if they could afford to do so. From some time into the term, when our tuckboxes were depleted, we were handed five shillings a week every Wednesday, until the end of term. Then we would run to the tuck shop to buy fresh bread or warm kabalagalas, the deep-fried pancakes made from sweet bananas and cassava flour. You had to hurry because there were two or three shops but only Juma's sold the best kabalagala and bread.

One Saturday, my friend Fiona and I wolfed a loaf of bread each for breakfast. We took our big plastic Tumpeco mugs to the dining room and filled them with black tea. Then we went to the dormitory, took out our bread and broke off pieces. We figured it would be easier if we did not slice it. Everyone looked at us in disbelief. I was fine afterwards but Fiona had an upset tummy. We never did that again.

On some Saturday nights we watched a film shown outside on the wall of the library. I saw *The Parent Trap* for the first time, sitting outside with a blanket, under the stars, wondering if the twins were going to get caught as they played tricks on their parents. It was magical. On other Saturday nights we had what the girls called a 'cow dance.' This was a dance party on the lawn of the headmistress's house. There were no boys, so girls danced with each other. I remember dancing to 'December, 1963 (Oh What a Night)' by Frankie Valli and the Four Seasons, 'Can't Get By Without You' by The Real Thing and a whole lot of Lingala tunes.

Sunday afternoon was visiting time and we all waited. Before I joined the school, when we visited my sisters, I would try to avoid signing the visitor's book because I did not have a signature. It was a source of agony and the big girls would tease me, insisting that I sign. To avoid them I would run as I got closer to the signing desk and would not stop until I reached my sisters' dormitory. We would sort out the signing on our way back. Now, as a student, I waited impatiently for someone to come down to Sherborne and say, 'Bakujidde!' (They have come for you). Or 'Where is Philippa? She's been bamjiddad.'

Gayaza had a tradition of singing and I loved singing. In primary school I was in the choir and I often went to the concerts of the national schools' music and drama festival with Maama. Gayaza always did well. At one particular concert, Vikki, who is now my sister-in-law, sang the song 'Bubbles'. She came walking onto the stage in her immaculate school uniform with these high platform block shoes. I was fascinated by this girl who was so confident and who was allowed to wear such shoes to school. And then she opened her mouth to sing: 'Bubbles of laughter, bubbles of …' I never forgot the song, or the person who sang it.

So in that term, when Miss Hobday, the music teacher, announced auditions for the Triple Singers, the junior choir, I announced in the dormitory that I would audition. May, who was about three years older, looked at me and burst out laughing. She said, 'The competition is high and I doubt you'll get in.' I looked at her and kept quiet. She didn't even sing herself. I practised the Italian folk song 'Marianina' hard. The audition was at Miss Hobday's house. I walked in, auditioned and was accepted. I ran back to the dorm to show off. What did May know? How I enjoyed being in the Triple singers. My favourite song was 'The Skye Boat Song':

Speed bonnie boat like a bird on the wing,
Onward, the sailors cry.
Carry the lad that's born to be king
over the sea to Skye.
Loud the winds howl, loud the waves roar,
Thunderclaps rend the air,
Baffled our foes stand by the shore,
Follow they will not dare ...

The harmonies were beautiful and the story captivating. I only sang with the Triple Singers for one term because at the end of that term we left the country.

Early in the first term, some of the Senior 2 girls took us under their wings to teach us about being boarders. They introduced us to what they called 'adves', or adventures. On our first 'adve', one Saturday evening, they took us to the chapel where a group of saved (born-again) Christian girls were meeting. The 1970s were a time of great revivals in East Africa. In the school there were the girls who went to chapel because they had to, those who did so because they came from Christian families, those who were 'saved' and then there were the bazukufu who were born-again and ultra conservative. They did not wear trousers or make-up or jewellery and they kept their hair short.

All this was new to me. We hid outside. The girls in the chapel moved out of the sanctuary into the vestry. The S2s signalled for us to keep quiet and we crept and stood underneath the vestry window. The girls in the vestry switched off the lights. Suddenly we heard a cacophony of voices – everyone in the room talking and praying all at once, in different languages – coming out of this darkened room. I was scared, I had never heard anything like that. The S2s told us that the girls were praying in tongues. 'If you disturb, then you will go to hell,' they said. Then they banged on the windows and ran away laughing. We followed them, terrified. When we got to the dormitory, they asked us, 'Couldn't you hear some of them saying the alphabet, and 'abracadabra'?' I don't remember what I heard.

The whole evening – the special group who greeted each other saying, 'Praise the Lord, Sister X,' the talking in tongues, the banging on the windows, the amusement of those who took us – disturbed me. I talked to God all the time – in nature, climbing my tree, watching a sunset and especially at dusk and when I sang. I believed that He had a plan for my life and that He was in control. I did not understand a relationship that made someone more special than others, that gave more access than others. God loved us all. I also felt guilty for banging on the windows and running away. High school was going to be tough, I thought.

A few Saturday evenings later, we passed the chapel again and one older student, Jean, called us and preached to us about going to hell. She was passionate and graphic. At one point she said: 'I wish Jesus would come now. Then he would take me to heaven. Yes, and I'd wave to you as I rose on the clouds to heaven and you sank down to HELL.' We were terrified, especially after knocking on the windows. We prayed with her and became saved. I didn't want to see Jean rising on a cloud as I sank down to Hell!

Being an old missionary school, Gayaza celebrated the significant days on the Christian calendar. Easter fell during the first term and the students did not get the weekend off. Instead they made it into a big celebration at the school. On Maundy Thursday we celebrated the Last Supper and the arrest of Jesus with song, prayer and Holy Communion. We filed out of chapel quietly at the end of the service, reflecting on Jesus' arrest and sacrifice for us all.

On Good Friday the choir put on part one of the Easter play. It ended with the Crucifixion of Christ, sombre and sad. Then came Easter Sunday. The school choir woke up early in the morning, before sunrise. They met in the chapel, covered in white sheets, each holding a candle, and walked all around the school from one dorm to the next, singing and gathering the crowd until the whole school, or a large number of us, all singing, were walking behind them.

I heard the singing getting louder and louder, so I dressed quickly and went out to join in. The grass was still wet with dew and the sun was just rising over the horizon. We followed them back to the chapel for a moving service celebrating the

Resurrection. I remember that breakfast being slightly better than usual. Later in the day, families came to visit and brought large meals for their children and their friends. Those who had a family in town shared with those who came from up country. I thought it was one of the most beautiful traditions of the school.

Death of the Archbishop

The drums beat
calling them to the chapel
that night.

One by one the girls streamed in

> *Abide with me*
> *Fast falls the eventide*

'Good evening girls,'
said the headmistress.
'We have heard
that his Grace the Archbishop,
and two government ministers,
were killed this afternoon.

In a car accident.'

Silence echoed loudly

against
the changing skies of the night.

'Minister Oboth Ofumbi
is the father of one of our girls.'

> *The darkness deepens;*
> *Lord with me abide ...*

The sound of sobbing
seeped through the chapel
like blood into the ground.

And as dusk faded,
darkness
thick with questions
ominous
unspoken
enfolded the girls.

'Let us pray.'

> *When other helpers fail.*
> *And comforts flee,*
> *Help of the helpless, Lord*
> *Abide with me.*

There was no prep that night.
Silently the girls trooped
down

to the dormitories
into a darkness
that swallowed all.

Maliza, Estella and I left Kampala shortly after the death of
Archbishop Luwum. The time leading to our departure is a blur
but I recall the night before we left. Our flight to Addis Ababa,
where we were to join my father, left at dawn so my mother
arranged for us to spend the night at the Speke Hotel and take
the shuttle to the airport.

I was excited to be going to see Daddy and spending the
night in a hotel then travelling by air, both for the first time. But
I felt apprehensive. The death of the Archbishop had changed
things. Although I did not know him personally, I was part of a
cohort of young people he had confirmed at All Saints Cathedral about two months before he was killed. I felt a strong
connection to him because of that. Although the media stated
that he had died in a car accident, all the overheard bits of conversation between adults were about murder.

We were taking the shuttle because it was not safe to travel
at that time of the morning. No one said anything, but I could
feel it. I was also anxious because only Maliza, Estella and I
were travelling. Maama, Fay and Chris were staying in Uganda.
I had no idea that they would be leaving too. I sensed that something big was happening, that our lives were changing, but I did
not know how.

The evening before we left we had dinner at home, for the last
time, and then Maama, Maliza, Estella and I went to the hotel.
We were woken up at 4am and hurried, groggy-eyed, to the

kombi shuttle. We drove to Entebbe in the dark. There were no incidents. Before long we were on the plane bound for Addis Ababa. Maliza had flown to Nairobi alone a couple of times, so I followed what she did. The air hostesses said something that sounded like, 'Kuvrash kuvratina', speaking in Amharic. Then: 'Welcome aboard Ethiopian Airlines flight ... to Addis Abeba ...'

Hours later, as the plane taxied down the runway in Addis, we looked outside, taking in the new sights. Then Estella cried, 'There's Daddy! Look at those legs. No one else has legs like that!' We looked outside and saw a tall man, who looked much like the Ethiopian people, with Daddy's legs. Daddy was double jointed so his legs curved slightly backwards. We did not believe it was him, but when we got off the plane, there he was meeting us. For close to a year now, he had been working with the African Association for Public Administration and Management (AAPAM), attached to the United Nations Economic Commission for Africa. Somehow, perhaps because of their attachment to the UN, and because we were children travelling unaccompanied from a troubled land, the protocol officer had got permission for him to meet us at the plane. We were so excited.

Addis was so different from Uganda. It smelt different. The air was cooler and there were fewer trees. Unlike Kampala, built on seven hills, Addis seemed to be built in a valley surrounded by hills. As we drove from the airport to Daddy's apartment, we noticed the hundreds of blue and white Fiats that drove up and down a wide road. Daddy said that those were the taxis. We would soon learn how to use them. There were other differences. The whole city would take afternoon siestas: everything would shut down for a few hours after lunch, then open up and work again until late. To us the siesta was a strange custom.

Daddy lived in a big apartment block in town. The apartment was spacious and smartly furnished. Different nationalities lived there, but I do not remember seeing anyone my age. The living room balcony faced a commercial college. Every evening, hundreds of well-dressed people arrived to study. The students milled around outside the gates, smoking, talking and catching up with friends until the school opened.

We sat on the balcony watching people come and go, and soon we got to 'know' some of the students and their friends. Estella and I created lives for them. 'There is that woman. She is looking for her friends. She can't see them sitting to the left. Can you see her?' We gave them names. We were fascinated that so many adults would come to school after work. We were also struck by how beautiful they all were.

It was good to be with Daddy. He took us around, helped us settle in. Then he told us that we would not be going back to Uganda. He said that Maama, Fay and Chris would be in Nairobi for a while and then join us in Addis. Maliza would be going to university in the States. Only Estella would have to go back to Uganda because she was in the last few months of her A Levels and it would be difficult to slot into another system. Looking back, I think that that must have been devastating for her.

In the meantime we were on holiday, with time to kill and not much to do. So Daddy enrolled us for French lessons. Early each morning we caught a blue and white taxi to the Alliance Française, each of us going to separate classes, and then met up and came home for lunch. Daddy had hired a young Ethiopian woman, Selamawit, to do the housework and cook. She would prepare lovely dishes for us. One day she made us fire-hot samosas. While she was making them she ate a whole chilli, the way we would eat carrots. She laughed at the look on our faces. We could not finish her fiery samosas and packed them for her to take home.

We visited Mercato, the largest open-air market in Africa. You could get anything and everything at Mercato, from spices to radios, food to clothes, livestock to beautiful jewellery. We had to get someone to guide us around and Daddy bought a beautiful gold necklace for Maama.

Addis Ababa was a tricky place in 1977. The Emperor Haile Selassie had recently died and President Mengistu Haile Mariam was in power. Many people believed that Selassie had been killed. There were still dissidents out there and it was not strange to hear gunshots during the day. I heard a visitor tell Daddy that 'everyone has a gun here.'

One day, after we got home from the Alliance at lunchtime, we heard gunshots. We went onto the balcony. The shooting was up the road and we saw people run and take cover. A few minutes later, when nothing more happened, everybody came out of hiding and went towards where the shooting had happened. We were scared, and found this response strange. Why go to the scene? What if there was more shooting? On that day Maliza had dropped Estella and me at the Alliance and gone sightseeing. She had made friends with an Ethiopian girl named Kirdst. We guessed they were together. She was not back when the gunshots went off so we were worried but she soon returned home unharmed.

Addis had more in common with Kampala than we had first thought. They also had shortages. Basics like bread and petrol were rationed. We learnt that, as foreigners working in an organisation connected with the UN, we had privileges that the locals did not have. We got petrol more regularly and we did not have to line up for bread.

5 New fires

There is magic in a dying fire!
The little blue flames that playfully
Hug the remnant pieces of wood
As if to tickle them into flame,
The ripe-red of the serene embers
In an unmatched beauty parade
Changing into other indescribable reds.
HENRY BARLOW

It was when we moved to Addis that I realised each city is different. It feels different, smells different and the light has a different quality. Its everyday life has its own rhythm.

There were coffee shops all over Addis. Tele Bar was the one next to the apartment building. The Ethiopians drank 'buna', a rich, dark coffee, from little cups. Standing on the balcony I watched people come, at any hour of the day, for their buna. It was often served to them in their cars, a new phenomenon to me. The waitress would come out, take the order, and return with a dark brew on a tray. Or the other drink they enjoyed: puréed pawpaw. Daddy thought this was a brilliant idea, given his love for pawpaws. I thought it was strange. Pawpaws were made to be eaten, not drunk.

We were used to having fresh milk or pasteurised milk with our tea. In Addis everybody we knew used powdered milk. We bought a brand called Klim, which tasted like milk and dissolved instantly. Instant milk: not in my wildest dreams had I imagined it.

We had always lived in a free-standing house but now we had to get used to the noises from the other flats. The woman in the flat above walked around in stilettos, making a click, click sound. My father took to banging the broom handle on the ceiling, following her around the flat. We followed behind him, laughing.

One day we saw a group of women in voluminous dresses squatting at the side of the road in deep conversation. We wondered what was going on. As they stood up, we realised they had been urinating at the side of the road, as men do. We were horrified, but it turned out that this was not an uncommon practice.

Soon we got news that Maama, Fay and Chris were safe in Kenya. They were staying in Ruiru, just outside Nairobi, on the farm of our family friends, the Kareithis. Now that we were all safe our parents had to decide what to do with us. Estella returned to Gayaza High School in Kampala, to finish the last few months of her A Levels. Maliza was accepted at Pace University in New York to study business administration, and she had a few months to kill before she left. I needed a high school to attend. I could not go to the local Addis schools because they were in Amharic and that meant learning a new language and a new alphabet. The only options in Addis were the American or the English school. My parents did not want me to change to the American system and expatriates in Addis said that the English school's standards were dropping as teachers were leaving. They always dreamt of returning to Uganda and so Kenya made the most sense, since the education system was similar. They felt it would be easier to find me a school if I was in Nairobi.

Maliza and I left Addis to join Maama, Fay and Chris. We stayed at the Kareithis in Ruiru for a while and then Maama found us a maisonette in Westlands, a reputable area of Nairobi. It was smaller than the kind of house we were used to, but pleasant, with a small garden. There were 16 maisonettes on the property, with a guard at the gate. It was close to the bus stop and the shopping centre was within walking distance. Right next to our maisonette stood the Hotel Intercontinental – a small hotel with a big name. Around this time, Maama managed to enrol me at Kenya High School, one of the more prestigious government schools, similar to Gayaza, except that it was not started by missionaries.

Living in Nairobi involved another change in lifestyle. We had to use public transport since we had no car or driver. Shopping meant buying only the necessary items or taking a taxi. We had good family friends, Eddie and Jean, who were students in Nairobi too. Their father, Uncle Nathan, and Daddy had been best of friends at university. They came to Nairobi on their own and used a particular taxi driver, Nganga, who worked in Westlands.

They introduced us to Nganga, who was a great help when we needed transport. Nganga was an old Kikuyu man with one leg that was shorter than the other. He took Maama to work every morning and brought her back in the evening. She was a teacher at Pangani Girls High School. He took Maama shopping. She found the buses difficult. Firstly, there was always a rush to get on and secondly, she was short and if she did not get a seat, she couldn't reach the rail to hold on comfortably. Most importantly, she needed to get home quickly because of Fay and Chris. Nganga was a godsend.

Every Sunday afternoon there was a concert at the hotel, in the garden next to the swimming pool. Estella and Maliza's bedroom looked right onto the pool so Fay and Chris, their caregiver Milicah, and I sat there on Sundays to watch the dancers and singers.

'Huli balulu bene,
ah ah ah, huli balulu bene,
ah, ah, efwe hururu mumbo
Huli balulu bene …'

They sang in Luhya, a language similar to Lumasaba, although I did not fully understand it. The drumbeats throbbed as I tried to copy the dance moves, their hips moving briskly from side to side, their raffia skirts following. That and the TV were our main sources of entertainment.

I started school a week before the exams. I had been on holiday for so long that my parents thought I should start as soon as possible and I was glad to be back at school. I was a day-girl, or day-bug as we were called, for those last three weeks of the second term of Form 1. I had never heard of a school that was both a boarding and day school. Most students were boarders.

On my first day, Maama and I drove to the school with Nganga. I was dressed in my grey skirt, white blouse, black and red tie, white socks and highly polished brown shoes. My heart was beating loudly in my ears.

As we approached the gate, I saw the tall stone dormitories curving backwards into the grounds and the crest of the school on the gate. I took in a quick breath. *Wow*, I thought. *Will I fit in?* Visions of experiences that the girls had in Enid Blyton's St Clare's and Malory Towers series flitted through my mind. It was either going to be a great experience or a terrible one.

I reported to the office, met the headmistress, Mrs Kariuki, and Janet was sent to fetch me and take me to my classroom. She was the class captain of 1K1 and we became fast friends. My class teacher was Mrs Albon, the wife of the deputy principal, who everyone called Papa. All the senior girls were in love with Papa and they could not understand why he had chosen her. She had pointy glasses and was plump. Her nickname was Macavity, because she was an English teacher who always taught the poem, 'Macavity the Mystery Cat', by T.S. Eliot. I stood out because I had joined the school so late in the year, and at breaktime the girls from other classes came to find out who I was.

I am new

'What tribe are you?'
asked the girl in a blazer.
I cocked my head to the side,
my brow creasing

as I looked at her
'I am Ugandan,'
as if that was a tribe
and before I could correct myself
I saw her interest fade.

'What sports do you play?'
asked another.
'None.' Their eyes glazed over.
I could have told them that I sing –
like a nightingale at that.
But singing is not a sport.
'Why did you come?' they asked.
I was thinking that too.
Before I could answer I
heard her voice.
'Do you remember me?'
I looked around,
standing in front of me
on tiptoes was
Maggi.
At the old school
I had waited for her
at the beginning of P6,
no one knew where she had gone.
Now, two years later,
she was here,
saving me.

After that first day, Fatuma, one of my classmates, showed me how the buses worked, but only on weekdays. Then, on the first Saturday we had a sports day and had to report to school early. I missed the bus I had hoped to take so I waited for the next bus to come but it did not. I got worried and started walking to school, following the route that the bus used. A couple of buses drove past me but I was not at a bus stop so they would not stop. I got to school hot, bothered and late, but when I told my classmates what had happened, they laughed. They explained to me how the buses worked on the weekends. I became a boarder in the third term.

Going to a new school meant getting used to the staff as well. I had some favourites.

Mrs Ayot

'Why are you new?'
she asked, looking at me over her glasses.
It was my first class with Mrs Ayot
and I had never met a teacher like her.
'What is your name?'
'Philippa.'
She turned to the girl
sitting at the desk in front
and said, 'Anjana, isn't it a coincidence?
I have a son called Philip.
He can be your boyfriend!'
she said to me.

By now the class had dissolved into giggles
and I wanted to run.

She taught history
like she had lived
with Napoleon and Mussolini
and fought with the Bolsheviks,
taking us on unforgettable journeys
through the ages.

Philip was much younger.
And who could complain when his mom
would call me to the staff room and say,
loud enough for all to hear,
'Philippa, Philip said hello.
And he sent you these sweets.'

Slowly I learnt to live
in this land away from home.

Finances were tight when we lived in Nairobi. Maama's job
paid the rent and Dad sent us living expenses. He sent money in
dollars but foreign exchange took three to four weeks to clear.
I never knew that. Maama was good at making sure we did not
feel the pressure of the move. At the end of the month, when
she got paid, or when Daddy's money came through, she bought
us something special for dinner, maybe roast chicken or duck.

At the beginning of the third term, when I had become a
border, there was no more catching buses and rushing. Maama
visited me every two weeks at school, with grub: Treetop Juice

(the orange cordial that was popular in those days), powdered and UHT milk, Milo, biscuits, bread and Blueband margarine. So although I did not have much pocket money, I always found something in my tuckbox. More importantly, my mother visited. Some of the girls had plenty of pocket money but rarely saw their parents, even though they lived in the same city.

Once, as the school holidays drew to an end, Maama sat me down and we spoke. The money Daddy sent had not yet been cleared. There was wasn't much money in the account. She asked me to make a list of the essentials for school and home. As soon as the money was cleared, she would bring me the rest.

Maama was going to work that Saturday so she gave me a cheque and the key to the postbox so I could collect the letters. I put them in my purse in my kiondo, slung it over my shoulder, and walked down to Westlands. I went to the bank first and then I went to the Uchumi Supermarket, bought a few things and put them in the bag. I went on, singing, to the next shop and picked up the rest of the things. When I got to the till, I could not find my purse. I emptied the whole bag and it was not there. I looked around, expecting to see someone holding it, but all I saw were irritated customers standing in line. I had to leave all my shopping and walk away, the eyes of the customers branding me the girl who could not pay for her groceries. I ran all the way home.

I had lost our last money. Finally home, I walked straight to my room and cried. I tried, between gulps of air, to explain to Milicah, but I did not make any sense. When Maama came home, I told her and she said, 'Stop crying and wash your face. We'll make a plan. Did you go to the post office and tell them our key has been stolen?' I said no. So she marched me down to Westlands Post Office where they sealed off our postbox. Then we went to the Indian butcher that Maama knew. She spoke to him and gave him a post-dated cheque for cash and we bought the remaining groceries. I even got a little pocket money.

What I missed most in Nairobi was family, especially my extended family. Without thinking about it I created another for myself and they brought joy and lightness into my life there.

My first family was of course Maggi's, a connection that has lasted to this day and expanded to our extended families. I discovered that they went to the same church as we did, St Marks in Westlands, so I never missed a Sunday during the holidays. This created an opportunity for her parents to get to know me, and for our parents to meet more regularly. So when they invited me to spend a half-term holiday with them I was so excited. I went to their house in Ngong Hills and met Maggi's five siblings: Chris, George, Robert, Christine and Maryanne. Chris, her older brother, was blind but a skillful piano player. We spent a lot of time singing ABBA and the Commodores.

The graciousness of the Kakomas was special. For a couple of half-terms they took me and three other Ugandan children, the Kawukis, into their home to join their six, so there were sometimes ten of us eating them out of house and home. Neither the parents nor the children complained, except perhaps when the noise became too much. Then Aunty or Uncle would give us some housework to do, or we would be told to do some schoolwork. If we were lucky, we would be told to go outside.

I loved the house in Ngong Hills. It was quite far outside of Nairobi, beyond the trading centre. A lone house with rolling hills as a backdrop, and nothing else. I loved the peace and quiet we woke up to, and because there was nothing much to do, we played, we sang and we went for long walks. We also had to wash our clothes. One half-term there was a water crisis. The water pipes were dry and we had to use the rainwater in the tank outside the house. We had to ration it, washing all our clothes in the same soapy water. We learnt the hard way that our mothers were right when they said to wash the white clothes first. Our whites came out a greyish, brownish white.

I called Maggi's mum Aunty Teddy Bear. Her name was Theresa, so most people called her Aunty Terry, but she was so warm that some of us called her Aunty Teddy. Maggi's dad was Uncle George to everyone else and Uncle Biba (short for Wilberforce) to me, because of a story he once told us about his childhood. Aunty was one of the few people who called me Namutebi, which I loved.

They were quite protective of us. One weekend, when we were about 17, Maggi and I were invited on a date to watch a movie. Charles and Jack were in the mixed choir we had with Lenana, a boys' school, and we enjoyed each other's company. Uncle Biba was not at all happy that we were going to meet boys. He preferred our friends to visit us at home. It took a lot of persuasion and the input of Aunty Teddy to convince him that nothing untoward would happen.

Aunty Irene, Maama's younger sister, and Uncle Mathias, her German husband, moved to Nairobi about a year after we did. He worked for the UN and after being stationed in what was then Upper Volta, now Burkina Faso, and at the UN Headquarters in New York, came to join the UN-Habitat office in Nairobi. Almost a year later, Maama, Fay and Chris moved to Addis to join Daddy, so Aunty's house became a home away from home for me. They often fetched me from school on exeats – the few Sundays when we were allowed to leave school for the day, or at half-term. When the term ended they took me to the airport so I could go to Addis.

Aunty's house was restful. She and Uncle Mathias introduced me to the music of Richard Clayderman, which became the soundtrack to my time there. That and the Bee Gees' *Spirits Having Flown* album. Aunty Irene loved cooking and her food was delicious. I even learnt how to eat prawns. After I turned 15, the legal age for drinking in Germany, they would offer me wine at the dinner table. I drank it sometimes, but alcohol never appealed to me. Sometimes we travelled out of Nairobi on day trips to places like Naivasha, or the Nairobi National Park. One day we went to the Nairobi Cinema to watch the movie *Fame*. I loved the music, I loved the dancing and I wanted to go to a school like that. St Clare's and Malory Towers faded into insignificance.

My other family were the Njoroges. In Form 1 I made friends with Irene, a serious girl with glasses. She was bright, she loved reading and music, and she was kind. One holiday she fetched me from our house in Westlands and took me to her home in Kamiti for the night. Her brothers, sister and parents soon became like family to me, especially after Maama, Fay and Chris moved to Addis.

When I was in Kamiti with the Njoroges, I was at home with my sisters and brothers; a teenager without cares. I didn't have to worry about Fay and Chris, or go to Westlands to do the shopping. Instead we went on little adventures on the farm. Allan, Irene's brother, would take the car and spin wheelies on the dirt road. Her father tolerated my endless chatter and singing in the car. Five years later, in our final year of high school, on Sundays after attending the service at St Andrews, we would borrow videos of the *Fame* TV series and buy ice-cream cones from Slush. With Irene I shared my deepest thoughts and fears. Her family's generosity, love and acceptance were grounding. To this day, 'Mum', Mrs Njoroge, still calls me Mwihaki, the Kikuyu name she gave me. It is a name I treasure.

During the July holidays in 1978, a year after we had moved to Nairobi, I came home and Maama took me to Biashara Street to buy an outfit. We got off the yellow Kenya Bus, as we called them, and down onto a street bustling with people. There were many Indian-owned shops where you could buy tea masala and spices – garam masala, turmeric, ginger and chilli – and pishori, the fragrant rice that Maama said was the best. There were the shops that sold clothes at affordable prices. I got a black pencil skirt with a small slit at the back and a metal buckle on the chain-link belt, a black and white polka-dot blouse and a pair of black 'going out' shoes. This was a rare treat, going out clothes. Then she told me that Jajja John and Jajja Maliza, my father's parents, were celebrating their fiftieth wedding anniversary and she had found someone who could take me to Kampala. I jumped up and down.

I travelled by road in a car full of adults I did not know. I was quiet most of the way. As we crossed the border into Uganda, I smiled as I saw the red soil and banana plantations along the way. How green it was. It rained and I breathed in the smell of the rain on the soil. I was home again. And then there were the roadblocks, too.

They dropped me at Uncle Jack's house, number 20 Akii Bua

Road, the road named after Uganda's first Olympic gold medal-list. Uncle Jack was the uncle who got on with everyone. He would play with the children and then you would see him with the old ladies, having a serious conversation, charming them with his smile. When we were younger, he would come to our home and sit on the sheepskin behind the sofa and tell us stories of Wanjovu, the elephant, who always made a huge poo. Or he would wrap one of Maama's special green napkins around his thumb, draw a little face on it and sing, 'Thumbelina, Thumbelina, tiny little thing, Thumbelina dance, Thumbelina sing ...' I loved Uncle Jack with all my heart.

Aunty Florence had a rich alto voice and a laugh like honey. She loved perfume. Later, when we returned to Uganda, she would stand behind us in church and Estella and I would whisper 'Aunty Florence', and sure enough, when we turned around, it was her. They had three children – Nakawungu, Anthony and Emmanuel. Nakawungu was about eight years younger than me but we had loved each other from the moment she was born. Anthony was hilarious. He was about three and knew that when his dad listened to the evening news he had to be quiet. As soon as he heard the jingle for the news, he would come to us and say, 'Sshh, amawule, amawule,' trying to say 'amawulire' (the news). Emma was a little younger and very quiet.

The celebrations took place in Salama, Munyonyo, where the Jajjas had their farm. We held a service at their local church. Jajja John wore a grey three-piece suit and Jajja Maliza wore a blue and white dress, with a short dress-coat and a hat. She wore shoes with a little heel and my aunties teased her about not being used to walking in them. They looked great.

We had a luncheon at their house at Munyonyo, with all the

food I had not eaten in a while: matooke, empombo, lumonde omuganda and ekyinyebwa – stews and sauces steamed in banana leaves, sweet potatoes, thick groundnut sauce. I was with the people I had missed; the whole extended family. We sat on mikeeka under the mango trees, like we used to do, listened to speeches, and cheered as the Jajjas cut their cake. It was great to be back in the womb of the family, even if only for a short while.

Estella had finished her A Levels and had been admitted to Makerere to study law. She was in Africa Hall and the weekend after the Jajja's ceremony I went to spend a few nights with her at the university. Her roommate was Viola, who had been a friend for such a long time she was and still is like family. That Saturday afternoon some guys came and invited them to go to Chez Josef, or 'Chezz', as it was called. There was an issue: I was only 14. But in the end they said I could go. I was so excited. It was my first time going to a disco.

They hired a 'special', a saloon car taxi. We were all dressed up and as we drove on Kampala Road we were stopped by the police for being in an overloaded car and taken to Central Police Station. This was terrifying because Central Police Station had a terrible reputation and anything could happen. We could have been thrown into prison, raped or killed. But the guys and the taxi driver negotiated; they paid a bribe, and off we went to Chezz. I had fun dancing and drinking Mirinda, much to the surprise of people who didn't know how young I was.

We left Chezz in the wee hours of the morning and then had the challenge of getting back into Africa Hall. It was late, and I think because of the political situation the girls had a curfew. They were not allowed to have visitors sleep over, so there was no way I was allowed in officially. We went to the bottom part of the hall and there was a wall made of blocks with spaces in between them. We put our feet into the gaps and climbed over slowly, being careful not to be seen or heard, and ran to Estella's room.

The incident with the police was something we were silent about for a long time. In times like those, you did not talk about potentially near-death experiences. We did not want to frighten our parents, but I think, more importantly, we did not want to be grounded for life.

Kenya High had great spirit. One area where this was expressed was in the support for the hockey team. When there was a home game, we all went to the fields, even the teachers, and some-times the matrons. When there was an away game, the team went in the kombi, while a busload of spectators followed. If the team won, Kamau and Daudi, the school's drivers, would take the bus and kombi around the school, hooting. We would pour out of the dormitories and celebrate. We had an unofficial agree-ment that if we were playing against any other school at Nairobi School or Lenana High School, our brother schools would sup-port us, and if they played at our school we would support them.

One year, both our school and Nairobi were in the inter-school semi-finals. Each team had to play two games – a home and an away game. Nairobi played their first game, against Jamuhuri High, at our school. At least half of Kenya High went down to the field to support Nairobi and they beat Jamuhuri. Then we played Loreto Convent Msongari at Nairobi, and the Nairobi boys supported Msongari! The team and supporters came back to school and told us what had happened, so a group of girls developed a plan – we knew what we had to do.

When the second Nairobi-Jamuhuri game at our school came around, the hockey team mobilised our whole school to be at the field. We went in droves, and cheered Jamuhuri. We asked Jamuhuri boys we did not know for their ties, which we wore in support, and Jamuhuri won. The Nairobi boys were angry and there were fights that day.

The following week we had to play our final at Nairobi. We knew we would have no support, so Mrs Wanjohi, our head-mistress, allowed two busloads of girls to go and support our team. And we won.

In the Kenya High kitchen there were two men who had great power. Mr Elam – or Mr 'Lamu', as he was known – was the oldest cook and it was advisable to be on his good side. Some-times, on a Saturday afternoon, if you went into the kitchen and helped out he would make you a cup of tea and give you cake. If he thought you were rude, you would never get any favours from him. He ran that kitchen.

There was Kipsii, a younger man with a broad smile from the Maasai or Kipsigis tribe. The girls found him attractive in a rugged sort of way. He did not have the clout of Mr Lamu, but he was a favourite because of the mischievous twinkle in his eye.

And then there was Jane Cook. Her official title was caterer. Cook was not her surname; it was the name we gave her. She was not popular, and became even less so on the night we decided to strike.

One Sunday evening as we walked into the dining hall for supper, we could smell something rotten. When the food was put on the table and the heads of the tables started dishing it out, we smelt that the minced meat was off. The kitchen staff had tried to disguise it by using a mound of curry powder.

One by one, the girls took the dishes back to the kitchen and spoke to Jane, but she just shook her head and disappeared from the kitchen. People started chanting and banging their cups on the table in the dining hall: 'We want food, we want food.' The chant grew louder and louder. One of the juniors from Mara, the house next to mine, was shouting loudly, jumping up and down, hitting her cup on the table. I had always thought that if I said 'boo' to her she would fall down, but the quietest girls seemed to be shouting the most.

The matrons tried to keep us quiet. Ms Nguri and Mrs Kamau, the two most powerful matrons, stood in front of us and rang the bell, but the girls shouted louder. The prefects tried, but no one was listening to them. Then Mrs Wanjohi, our headmistress, walked into the dining hall. She was a small woman who wore big glasses. She stood in front of us and stared. She did not say a word, did not make a gesture. She just stood there and within seconds the dining hall was silent.

'What is going on?' she asked. We all started to speak at once. She raised her hand and we fell silent again. Then she called on one of the prefects and said, 'Tell me, what is going on?' She listened and then asked for a plate of food. She sniffed it and nodded her head. We all roared in delight. Then she told the kitchen staff to make us more food – dengu (green lentils) and bread – and went on to lecture us about the best way to deal with a problem.

I can still see her, standing in front of about 700 shouting girls; her stillness, listening and quick decision-making. She was a fine role model.

The greatest gift for me, at Kenya High, was the choir. In Form 2, Miss Mary Cole, an American Peace Corps volunteer, arrived to teach music. It was like striking a match in a pile of dry firewood. Miss Cole was driven and even more so because her greatest rival, we got to learn, had been sent to teach at Alliance, a school that had a well-established music department. Miss Cole set out to make ours even better.

She auditioned people and in a short time we had a large choir. The Peace Corps was organising a regional meeting in Nairobi and she got our choir chosen to perform. We sang an arrangement of Martin Luther King's 'I have a dream' speech, as well as traditional songs. We worked *hard*. You had to come to choir practice with a pencil so that you could mark your music sheet. If you were late for rehearsal three times, you were kicked out. She picked out strong singers in each voice section and if your section was off, she would call you out. We started taking responsibility for the people around us.

On the day of the performance we needed two busloads to get the choir to the Kenyatta International Conference Centre. Our uniforms and hair had to be perfect and our shoes polished; Miss Cole checked. We stood in front of a room full of Americans and sang. At the end they stood up and clapped and clapped. We were overjoyed.

The following term we had a choir of 200 girls, so rehearsals moved from the music room to the dining room. She announced that the whole school would sing the national anthem in three-part harmony for speech day. Sometimes she would stand in rehearsals and say, in her Southern drawl, 'Askin' me to teach the whole of Kenya High to sing the national anthem in three-part harmony is like askin' me to walk on water!' We would roll our eyes, thinking. *Who asked you to do this?* We entered the Kenya National Music Festival every year and won.

We learnt so much about music from Miss Cole and when she left two or three years later, we carried on with the things she had taught us. Four years later, in my final year of high school, we had a music teacher who informed us that she was not entering the choirs in the festival. 'I am a piano teacher and I will only be entering my piano students this year.' We called an emergency meeting and agreed that we would teach and conduct the choirs. All she needed to do was enter us in the festival and make sure the fees were paid.

Both the junior and senior choirs would each enter the set piece and the traditional piece. Jackie, Irene, Maggi and I worked with the senior choir. We divided the girls into their voice parts, and for the first few weeks we practised in different venues. Jackie took the first sopranos in the lecture theatre. She had perfect pitch and could sight-read like a wizard. She did not need a piano. I took the second sopranos, Maggi the first altos and Irene the second altos. We were spread between the music room, chapel and dining hall.

Mr Munday from the neighbouring boys' school, Lenana, invited us to sing in a mixed choir and wrote an original composition for our senior choir. It was in Kiswahili and it was syncopated, with a jazzy beat. We worked so hard that term. Mr Munday was invaluable back-up. He would sometimes come to our rehearsals in the evenings and was always ready to give us advice. Jackie conducted the set piece and I conducted the original composition. In the end we won several prizes. It was one of my greatest achievements.

The following term, as we prepared for speech day, a new music teacher from England, Mr Floyd, joined the school. His skin was pale and he blushed so easily that we secretly called him Pink Floyd. The original composition was the piece chosen for speech day and Mr Floyd was conducting it. He did not have the feel of the piece and had not yet established a relationship with the girls. After a few rehearsals, the girls said to me, 'Philippa, you have to conduct. It's the only way we will get it right. Talk to Pink Floyd, please.' So I spoke to him and he agreed.

My last speech day at Kenya High was the best. As I stood up to conduct, my eye caught a movement at the side door. It was my mother. She had flown in from Uganda without telling me and arrived in time to see me conduct the choir. The girls sang like angels. Then, for the first time in my six years at the school, I won not one but two prizes: the general paper prize – the compulsory general knowledge subject – and the music prize. It was the first time in my time there that the music prize was won by someone other than the music prefect.

Jajja Jelly

Muzukulu wange Firpy
she wrote.
Her salutation
brushed away
my homelessness
proclaiming me as
her own.

Her words scrawled
across the page,
my name spelt
like only she did.
Jajja Maliza had written
to me,
a letter.

I could see her squinting at the page
as she wrote
in the cool of her house in Munyonyo,
outside the cattle lowing,
the mangoes ripe on the trees,
a breeze tickling the leaves,
Jajja John sitting in his armchair
on the veranda.

Miles away in Nairobi
as I read it again, and again,
I tasted the mangoes, sweet,
wiped the juice dripping down my chin,
I smelt the cows.
I heard her call for
someone to switch on the radio.
I felt the lake breeze kiss my skin
as I caressed
her soft upper arms,
shaking, like jelly.
Her words

drawing me against
her big bosom,
rooting me,
home.

On the 11th of April 1979, Amin was overthrown. I was in Addis
Ababa with the family during the Easter holidays when we
heard the news. For weeks Maama and Daddy had the radio
locked onto the BBC. When we heard the news, we started
jumping up and down and shouting. Maama picked up the
phone and called some other Ugandans and their friends. They
all decided that we must go and take over the embassy so we
climbed into the cars and off we went. The adults took the keys
from Peter Otai, who was then Ambassador, someone made
speeches, and then we sang our national anthem.

Oh Uganda, may God uphold thee
We lay our future in thy hands
United free, for liberty
In peace and friendship we'll live.

We went through the building and took down all the pictures
of Idi Amin. Maama and some of the ladies took one of the pictures outside, asked for matches and we tried to set it alight. It
only burnt at the edges, and Maama said, 'He is going to live
long. Even his picture refuses to burn!' Amin went on to live in
Saudi Arabia until August 2003.

The period after Amin was overthrown was a time of great
change and political unrest. On April 13th 1979, Yusuf Lule was
appointed president. He was seen as someone who would unify

the country. Sixty-eight days later he was asked to relinquish his position and was replaced by Godfrey Binaisa, who was in power for almost a year.

It was around this time that the Bigirwenkyas – Aunty Flora, my father's sister, and her husband Uncle Big, one of my father's best friends from University – were back from the States with our cousins. It was the first time in six years that they had been back home. Daddy went to Kampala for a visit, and possibly to prepare for our return. For the first time in years Jajja John and Jajja Maliza had all their children together. They took a family photograph under the big mango tree in front of the Jajjas' house. It was the last family photo they took.

6 *And there are ashes*

Sorrow is like a precious treasure, shown only to friends.
AFRICAN PROVERB

Ashes

The end of a life echoes loudly.

Even when death is expected.

Silence reverberates where once the rhythmic beat of heart,
the vibration of voice, the pulse of breath sounded.
Cold filling up the spaces where love-fire once forged lives
      together –

and there are ashes.

Grief takes hold – an unyielding hand, pushing you face-first
        into the gritty bed of ashes.
You fall in and the greyness enshrouds you,
mouth filled with dust.
Eyes blinded with ash-filled tears you lie there, fingers raking
        through the debris.

And then slowly, imperceptibly, you find embers.
Small inconsequential bits from the love-fire that once burnt.

As you coax these embers to life,
grief fingers release their grip
and the love-fire shows you that
there are things even death cannot take away:
        the blood that flows through your veins – your voice
                that is her voice, that walk that is his walk, that
                mind that questions like hers, that heart that
                loves like theirs –
There are things death cannot erase:
        that smile, that look, that touch,
        those words,
        that moment …
Yes, things death cannot mend:
        wounds, bruised hearts, unspoken words –

The end of a life echoes loudly.

And there are ashes.

We had barely moved to Nairobi when we got the news that Khukhu, Maama's mother, had passed away. We were a family scattered to four countries and my mother agonised about going to her mother's funeral.

Going home

Maayi.
At the dining table
shoulders hunched.
Quiet tears.
A moan.

Two aunties next to her,
hushed words,
taut faces.

A child
leaning against the wall,
eyes flashing, fists clenched.
'What did they say?'

Maayi turns,
'I'm all right.
Khukhu passed away last night.'

The child
wraps her arms

around her Mother
mourning her Mother.

Maayi,
dislocated.
Far away from
home where dread
locks, imprisons,
silencing,
scattering, shattering.
Alone
with three of her children.
The older two
wheelchair bound.
Minds alert
unable to speak, walk,
or care for themselves.
The younger one, 13.
The caregiver barely 19.

She must go.
Can she leave the children alone?
Bury her Mother.
Will she be safe?

Her husband
kilometres away,
her eldest child further.
The second-born at home –
maybe she will be at the funeral.

Aunty speaks.
'What if the soldiers get you? Stay.'
Maayi stands.
'I must go.
I must bury my Mother.'

Bag packed.
She gives the child money.
'I'll be back soon.
If you need anything
call Aunty.'

Maayi travels
through the Rift Valley
towards Busia.
Heart shattered.
Dread and courage
side by side.
Home calling.
Home pushing.
Calling, pushing, pushing, calling –

She remembers
the last words her mother spoke.
Hand on her cheek, she asked,
'Fayce, will you manage
with the children in a foreign land?'
She looked at her mother
and said, 'Maayi, Were kana akhuliinde.'

God will take care of us.

Maayi crosses Manafwa,
the river of her home.
The floodgates open
washing over her.

At the homestead
they wait.
Coffin lowered into
the grave.
They wait.
Corrugated iron sheets over
the grave.
They wait.

Maayi.

As the sun sets
she steps out of the car
into the homestead.
She is here.

The voice of an old woman
singing a dirge
rises through the air.
One by one
they move,
as if dancing,
to the grave.

Maayi is here
to bury her
Mother.

It was lunchtime at Kenya High School, on the 19th of July 1979. After grace had been said, we waited for any announcements. I heard the prefect say, 'Can Philippa Barlow report to Mrs Wanjohi's office immediately after lunch.' My heart sank. All through lunch I tried to imagine what I might have done wrong that week. In previous weeks, a group of us had been having problems with Miss Cole the music teacher and we'd had to go to the office, but that had been sorted out. I hurried through my lunch, straightened my tie, tucked in my shirt and walked to the office. A couple of friends caught up with me and asked me what I had done, but I had no answer.

When I got to the office someone was with Mrs Wanjohi so I sat in the secretary's office until she let me in. 'Ah, Philippa,' she said. 'Please sit down.' I sat down thinking it must be serious. We made small talk and then she asked me if I knew a Dr Jack Barlow in Uganda.

I smiled and said, 'Yes. He's my dad's brother, my favourite uncle.' I thought, *Maybe Uncle Jack is in Nairobi and he's coming to see me.*

Then she told me, 'He was killed last night.' Shot, she said, but she did not have any more information. All I knew was that they had killed Uncle Jack. Everything else became a blur. I could not stop crying. She let me sit there for what felt like hours. Then the bell rang for classes. She said, 'You can go down to the dormitory to rest. I'm really sorry for your loss.' I walked away from the office, the corridors emptied of girls, down to my boarding house, where the matron let me in.

The dorm was silent. I sat on my bed looking at the other empty beds, 18 of them. I covered myself with the bedspread and cried myself to sleep, all the time thinking that Mrs Wanjohi had got it wrong. Uncle Jack was a dentist, not a politician or a soldier. Uncle Jack got on with everyone. He was such a gentle dentist, with a sense of humour. He made going to the dentist fun. I did not believe that anyone would want to kill him. Maybe, I thought, it got so dangerous for him that they had faked his death, smuggled him out in a petrol tanker like I had heard they had done for someone else. Maybe, when I woke up, he would be here visiting me.

I was woken after four when school ended and my friends came looking for me. As I told them it began to sink in. This was not a bad dream.

That evening a group of us went for choir practice at the St Andrews church like we always did on Thursdays. Aunty Irene, my mother's sister, and Uncle Mathias came over to see me and told me what had happened. My little cousin, Nakawungu, my favourite little cousin, had also been shot – in the leg. She had begged the men not to kill her daddy and they had shot her. She was in hospital. I hated Idi Amin. I hated all those State Research men and the soldiers. I hated the people who had taken over from Amin – the killings felt even worse and more brutal. Who would shoot a child? When would they stop?

Weeks later I was back in Addis Ababa for the school holidays. Our cousin Norah Bigirwenkya was visiting too. Her family had been back in Uganda, for the first time since they left for the States, when Uncle was killed. Her brothers, Hosea and

John, tall teenage boys, had been at his house that night. Luckily the gunmen did not see them.

One morning, Estella, Norah and I all woke up crying. 'What's wrong?' someone asked.

'I am just so sad,' I replied.

We all got into one bed and spoke for hours, about our lives in these foreign lands, about our losses, about Uncle's funeral. We laughed and cried, a box of tissues on the bed between us. Daddy peeped in, probably to wake us, gave a wry smile and closed the door.

Years later, I learnt about the events that led to his murder. It was during the rule of Godfrey Binaisa, a period when the cracks between Ugandans who had worked together to get rid of Amin were beginning to show. Many medical personnel were killed and harassed, but no one knew who was doing it. Nurses had been raped by soldiers in the nurses' hostel, ward maids shot on their way home one evening, and some doctors were killed. Uncle Jack was part of a team of medical personnel who met with the head of the military commission, Paulo Muwanga, to demand that something be done to protect them. They also asked that the soldiers who had raped the nurses be brought to book, because they had records of their names and identity numbers. When they were told there was nothing that could be done, Uncle Jack challenged the government. The doctors went on strike, and the next day Uncle was killed.

We returned to Uganda in 1981, and it was bittersweet. It was great to be back home with family, but life had changed. There was no peace. There had been a general election in December 1980, but the results were contested. The Uganda People's Congress, led by Obote, was declared the winner, amidst many accusations of rigging. Museveni's Uganda Patriotic Movement was said to have lost. They went into 'the bush' and started a civil war that lasted six devastating years. The nights were riddled with gunfire – 'popcorn disco' was what people called it – and dogs howled like people crying. We had left a place where we slept peacefully at night to return to a home filled with fear.

We stayed in Aunty Florence, Uncle Jack's widow's townhouse. There must have been at least twelve of us, including the children, staying there. After a few weeks, our furniture started arriving – one, sometimes two crates a week, because there was only one direct flight from Addis to Entebbe. It came on Wednesdays. When we moved into our new home at no. 5 Sezibwa Road, opposite my old primary school, we played a guessing game every Wednesday: 'I wonder what will come today?' In the first few weeks all we had were our beds, some cutlery and curtains. Aunty Florence cooked for us and my father collected our dinner on his way home from work. We ate upstairs because we only had curtains for the upstairs windows. I would take the tray of plates downstairs.

I was 17 then. I descended the stairs into the darkness, and as I switched on the dining room lights, the floor crawled with huge cockroaches that scurried and hid. I rushed into the kitchen, not sure which was greater: my fear of being exposed to the evil people outside by the light in the curtainless house, or my terror at the cockroaches. I put the tray down, switched off the lights, and hurried back upstairs. I was so glad when Maama called in the fumigator.

One evening, the gunshots were so close you could see them light up the sky like fireworks. I helped Maama and Daddy drag our mattresses into their room, and Fay, Chris and I huddled together on the floor. I cried myself to sleep.

I asked Daddy why we had come back for this, but as time went on I understood that, for my parents, living outside of Uganda indefinitely had never been an option. They had always planned to come back. They loved Uganda. When Daddy was offered the job of head of the civil service, he took it. It was his chance to help rebuild the nation. This was our home.

But, once again, many young graduates left Uganda in the 1980s. They went to Lesotho, Botswana and the South African homelands, this time around looking for better economic prospects. I left in 1988 to join my boyfriend, Victor, who was working as a doctor in Lesotho.

On 28 December 1990, Victor and I got married in Uganda. We were living in Namibia at the time and planned our wedding from a distance. We made suggestions and our families and friends in Uganda made it happen. I had just started working as a lecturer at Ongwediva College of Education, and he was a doctor at the Oshakati State Hospital. Our wedding was a lovely, brief moment with all of our families and friends together again.

My father had built a semi-detached house near to their first home in Muyenga. They were living in one house with my sisters and brother, and because they were between tenants in the other, I was using it over the wedding period. I remember dressing up on my side, and then running into Maama and Daddy's house to show Fay and Chris what I looked like. Fay smiled her approval and stroked my dress. She loved beautiful things. She and Chris came to the church service at All Saints

Cathedral and were part of the wedding photos. This was such a blessing for me.

We returned to Oshakati soon after, and a few weeks later I had to travel to Windhoek to sort out my work permit. It was 800 kilometres away, and I thumbed a lift with a Finnish doctor friend of ours, Juha, who worked near Oshakati. His family lived in Windhoek and he was going for a few days of leave. We left on Wednesday the 6th of February. He offered me a place to stay as well, for which I was grateful.

Early in the morning, on the 7th of February, as I prepared to go to Home Affairs, Juha's wife knocked on the door of my room. I had a phone call from Victor. He told me that my sister Fay had passed away that morning, from complications with pneumonia. She was 30 years old.

I hung up. I felt as if the world had stopped. Later, I phoned Victor back to confirm what he had told me. I phoned home too, to speak with my parents. I did not know what to do. I couldn't go home for the funeral. It was so soon after the wedding and money was tight. To make matters worse, my work permit had not yet been issued because the office in Oshakati did not send the final paperwork through to Windhoek in December as they had promised. My December and January salaries had not been processed because of the work permit. I had gone to Windhoek to sort it out, and now this.

I put my grief aside and went to the Home Affairs office to sort out my problem. Around noon, after standing in many lines and walking between Home Affairs and the Department of Education, I was told that my application was late and there was nothing that could be done. The guidelines for employing foreigners had changed in January, and I would have to reapply for my job. I felt as if my world was crashing in on me. I asked to see a manager, and he said that only the permanent secretary could assist me; that is, if I could get an appointment with him. So I went to his office and asked to see him. I knew that I would not be able to make it to my sister's funeral, but I was going to make sure this would not be a problem again if anything else happened.

I explained to his assistant that my application had actually been made the previous year, before the new laws, and there was an outstanding document that Oshakati had not sent through. I believed the new guidelines did not apply to me. The assistant said that the permanent secretary was going to a meeting and would not be able to see me until next week. I said I would wait for him to return, and would not leave until I had seen him. Oshakati was too far away. I sat and waited.

At 4pm he got back and she told him that I had refused to leave. We spoke and he said I was right, and then he signed my papers. He picked up the phone and told someone to process my document, and the next morning, before we drove back to Oshakati, I got my work permit. Ten hours later, in my house in Oshakati, I broke down and wept for the sister I had lost.

A month or two later I found out I was pregnant and our daughter Faye Victoria Katiiti Khakasa was born on the 7th of November 1991. One day in 1986, years before we got married, as we sat on the stairs in front of my piano room, Victor had asked me what we should call our first child. I looked at him, dumbstruck. I had not thought about getting married or having children. He was just my boyfriend then. He said we should call our first child Fay. I said okay. The name had much more meaning when Faye was born.

For many years after my sister's passing I often felt her with me, laughing at me, spurring me on when I was about to give up, reminding me to believe that things would be okay.

On the 11th of September 1995, our son Senteza Moses was born at Panorama Mediclinic in Cape Town. We had been living in Cape Town since 1993. Victor was training to be a specialist physician at Tygerberg Hospital, and we lived in the doctors' quarters at the hospital. Faye was four years old and thrilled to be a big sister. Maama was unable to come and be with me for Senteza's first six weeks of life because she was looking after Chris and my father, so my mother-in-law, Maama Eva, came like she had done in Oshakati. It was good to have motherly support in our cramped little flat in the doctors' quarters.

Almost three months after Senteza was born, on the 9th of December, we got a call to tell us that Chris had passed away. He had been in hospital for a few weeks with bronchopneumonia, but no one had told me. They had kept quiet to protect me because I was still nursing Senteza. Chris was 33 years old.

I was devastated: about his death, about not knowing that he had been sick, and about being so far away. And I was unable to go to the funeral. Sente was too small and finances were tight. I was grateful that we had been able to go to Uganda for Easter that year and spend a few weeks at home. Faye was old enough by then to interact with her Uncle Chris and not be afraid of him.

This time I felt keenly the dislocation of grieving in a place where no one knew the person I had lost. Life continued around me as if nothing had happened, and yet I'd lost my only brother and given birth to my son. There wasn't much time for grieving, so I thrust myself into taking care of Senteza, and helping Faye adjust to being a big sister.

The year 2006 was when my parents and parents-in-law were to celebrate their fiftieth wedding anniversaries. My in-laws had planned a big ceremony at the end of June. My parents were to celebrate on the 1st of September. They kept saying they did not want a big celebration. During Lent that year, the priest in my church spoke about how God lavishes us with love. I suddenly wanted to lavish my parents with love. I began speaking to my sisters and my cousins about a way in which we could do this.

In June, we went home to Uganda, to celebrate with my parents-in-law. I had spent time praying that year – for my family, for peace, for wisdom and because of this sense that a dam was about to burst. Daddy, who had turned 77 in May, was healthier than we had seen him in years. He even danced at my in-laws' party. I remember my daughter Faye saying, 'I have never seen Jajja Henry so well.' He would sit at the dining table in the mornings and write a to-do list. She found this hilarious. My eldest sister was in hospital and was happy with the doctor who was treating her. The family support system had kicked in, and she was doing well. There was a calm at home and I left feeling happy. The plan for a small family gathering, a love feast, was underway.

Ten days later Maama called to say that Daddy had fallen and broken his hip. She phoned me almost immediately. This was not what she would normally do. Usually when there was a problem at home they went to hospital and I was informed later when they knew what was going on. I was concerned about this but it seemed as if everything was under control. Maama had support, and he had been so healthy when we saw him that I did not worry.

A few nights later I had a dream. I heard a voice saying to me, 'Philippa, he is going. You have to let him go.' I woke up in tears and I prayed it wasn't true but the feeling stayed for a day or two. I prayed that if this was so, that I would be able to say goodbye. In the weeks that followed I phoned home regularly. Initially I got the sense that things were going well. Whenever I spoke to Maama or Dad, they would say, 'Abaantu nga batwaagala! Twali tetumany nti batwaagala bwebati': We did not know that people loved us this much. Family and friends were well and truly lavishing them with love.

But a sense of worry crept in. Weeks passed and they had still not operated on his hip. They thought he had a blockage in his intestines and operated on his stomach, leaving his hip untouched. After about four weeks, I felt the urgent call to go home. A phone call from my cousin Sophie and my god-mother, Aunty Winnie, followed this. I prepared to leave and started getting things that he needed, such as a food supplement not available in Kampala, and a special mattress to prevent bed sores, not available in Mulago Hospital.

When I arrived at Entebbe, the first person I saw was Maama Eva, my mother-in-law, and for a moment I thought I was too late. She smiled at me, gave me a hug and said, 'Webale kujja.' Thank you for coming. Then I saw Estella, and Bukenya, my parents' driver. Maama Eva had come to the airport purely to support me. I was touched and knew I was not alone.

Later that evening I went to Mulago Hospital, up to the sixth floor, to the VIP room reserved for current and retired senior government officials, where my father and mother were. At some point, I am not sure when, it had become imperative for a patient in hospital in Uganda to have a helper, usually a family member, by their side at all times. Maama had been by his side since he was admitted to the hospital. We all knew that she would not leave. She looked tired and Dad was weak. My cousin Mire, or Reverend Diana, as she is known professionally, was with them and when I said I would spend the night, she offered to go home and get me a mattress. I stayed there until he passed away a week later.

The VIP room

'The builder of the nation is dead.
But he was old,'
they said.

On the 6th floor, in the VIP room
of our national flagship hospital
He lay.
Six weeks
he waited for his hip to be fixed
only to be
buried with it untouched.

'The builder of the nation is dead.
But he was old,'
they said.
Waiting three days
for the physician
to say 'His heart is okay, you can fix his hip'
and then have the surgeon disappear
to a conference, they say.

His health ebbed away,
as he lay on his back.
Then his stomach ached.
So they cut him open
and stitched up his gut,
his hip still untouched.

'The builder of the nation is dead
but he was old,'
they said.

On the 6th floor, in the VIP room
of our national flagship hospital
he lay.
'Here, take this blood
quick to that lab in town.'

We rushed around, vials of blood in our bags
to get the results they needed.
There is a lab
in the flagship, you know,
but mostly it does not work.

Results in hand
we rushed back to the room
but the doctor only returned the next day.

The head nurse refused to give
sterilised hospital bedding,

'Washing machines destroy them, you know.
Ward X has none left, for they used the machines –
but I still have all my sheets!'
I looked at the nurse who started
her ward round at 11, and
took blood samples hours
after the doctor's request.
Bile rose inside
but as I opened my mouth to speak
someone said,
'Don't antagonise the nurse.
Be grateful that she is here.'

'The builder of the nation is dead.
But he was old,'
they said.
In the VIP room, on the 6th floor, of our
national flagship hospital
we loved him and prayed for him.
It was all we could do,
impotent against a system
that made us grateful for crumbs.

Slowly he slipped away.

He vomited all last night
(in the VIP room on the 6th floor
of the national flagship hospital),
but the nurses would not come.
'Too many patients,' they said.

'And at least you are here.'

As the sun drew over the horizon
his vomit turned to blood
and still no nurse.
So we took out our phones
and called the doctors we knew.
'Please come,' we cried,
to the VIP room, on the 6th floor
of our national flagship.

Off to ICU
and still no sterilised sheets.
'Bring his blankets and pillows too.
And take off your shoes when you come in!'

Early Sunday morning
the ward phone rang.
This time a nurse came round the door.
'They want one of you to go
to ICU,
they need to talk to you.'
I hurried and dressed
for I am young and quick
and when I entered
I saw
The builder of the nation gone.

And his nation staggers along.

In early May 2009, I stood in my study, five months pregnant with my youngest child. I was getting ready to go to the radiologist for a scan to make sure that my baby was fine. I felt overwhelmed. I was almost 45, my blood pressure was high, Faye was in matric, we still hadn't sorted out her dress for the matric farewell, I was wondering whether Sente was in the right school, Victor was still coming to terms with the pregnancy, and I was still grieving my father.

Holding a letter from my gynaecologist to the radiologist, I decided to read it. My eyes were immediately drawn to the large XY on the page and I knew it was a boy. In that moment, I felt my father standing beside me on my left, my brother Chris sitting high up on my right; behind them my late grandfathers and uncles. Chris was laughing with his head thrown back like he always did, and my father said, 'Receive this child. It will be all right.' I was overcome with peace. I named him Christopher Henry Kutosi.

One day in February 2012, my mother phoned me and asked, 'Ojja ddi okundaba?'[7] It wasn't a question. It was a summons. I bought a ticket and went to visit her in March. Her sight was deteriorating and she wanted me to help her sort out a few things. I did what I could in two weeks and we spoke about my going back later in the year.

In the afternoon on Good Friday, about ten days after I had returned to Cape Town, Estella called me and told me they were taking Maama to hospital. 'She had a runny tummy, and chest

---

7. When are you coming to visit me?

pain too.' Maama had a heart condition and was on medication but she was such a strong, self-contained person that few people understood that she was not well. I rang Estella later that evening and they said she was being admitted to the ICU. I could not speak to her because she was with the doctor. I called again and tried to speak to her but she said she was in too much pain and so I said I would call later.

I woke up at 4am, unable to sleep, and said to Victor, 'Maama is going.' I could not explain why, but I knew. He did not say much. I was filled with a range of emotions – glad that I had been able to spend two weeks with her recently, sad that I was not there to care for her, torn because when I had called her the day before she was in too much pain to speak. I left my bed and went down to my study to work, but I could not do anything. I tried to pray. I tried to sing, but could do nothing.

About an hour later the phone rang. It was Estella, telling me that Maama was dead. I sat still for a while and my eyes filled with tears. She who had taken care of all of us, held us all together, taught us how to rise, and rise again, no matter how hard the knocks, was gone. Alone in the ICU of a hospital, with no one who she loved there to say farewell. She had waited till they all went home and then she passed. I walked upstairs slowly, crying, to our bedroom and told Victor.

We spoke to the children and then I called my cousins in South Africa, and my cousin who was Maama's goddaughter, in Rotterdam. I prepared for the journey home. Our Ugandan community in Cape Town came to our home that evening to pay their respects and offer support. Outwardly, I think I appeared all right – not many tears – but inwardly I was all over the place. It was as if I had lost my centre of gravity. There were signs, like misplacing my phone. When I took my clothes out of the washing machine to hang them up, there it was – dead. Or pulling out the suitcase and not knowing what to pack. The next morning, Easter Sunday, as I got ready to go to the airport, I changed my clothes three times. What do you wear on your way home to bury your mother? I finally wore a pair of jeans.

I thought about Maama as Victor drove me to the airport. Her faith was practical and private. Outside of church, we did not often pray together when I was growing up. She believed that your relationship with God was between you and God. As she aged, she said she prayed to God every day that she would not linger, that she would go quickly. At our last supper together in March 2012, my sister Estella asked that we pray. She shared a Bible reading. Maama looked at us and said quietly, 'You know, I still pray for miracles.' We prayed and said goodnight.

As I walked to the check-in counter at Cape Town International Airport, the envelope with my passport, my yellow-fever vaccination certificate and ticket fell down and everything spilt out. I bent down to pick them up and went to check in. As I left the counter and moved towards the gates, I opened the envelope to find my yellow fever vaccination certificate. The bright yellow book was not there. I walked around the check-in area looking for it. I was starting to panic. I approached one of the airline ground staff. Had someone picked it up and handed it in? Then we both saw one of the cleaning ladies holding a yellow document. I ran up to her and asked to see it. It was mine. I was so grateful I almost hugged her. Then I put the yellow certificate into the envelope, into my handbag, tucked the bag firmly under my arm and walked to the gate.

There was a hollowness in my body. I felt as if I was dragging myself, as though, if I did not hold myself together, I would disintegrate, be blown away by the wind, and then I would not know how to put myself together again.

On the plane I sat between two men. I wiped away tears from time to time, staring straight ahead. I felt them sitting stiffly next to me, their eyes brushing over me awkwardly with furtive glances, but I did not have the desire to explain. Especially since no one asked.

How do you share with someone the loss of a mother they did not know? How could they understand the immensity of my tiny Mother?

In Johannesburg I bought a replacement phone and checked in at International Departures. The trip from Cape Town had been the longest I had ever known and I thought I would get lost when I arrived at O.R. Tambo, even though I knew it well. In the departure lounge in Johannesburg, I was afraid that I would lose something again. I barely had the strength to get myself onto the plane. For the first time I understood the saying in Luganda: Amaanyi gaampwedde mu – I felt as if my spirit had drained out of me. I decided to have a head and shoulder massage. All I had to do was sit in one place for 30 minutes. I could not get lost or lose anything if I sat in one place. So I did it.

I got to Entebbe safe and sound and my nieces Elsa and Michelle, and Bukenya, Maama's driver, were there to meet me. It was odd not to have her meet me at the airport. The only time I remember her not fetching me was when Daddy was in hospital in 2006.

We got through the endless traffic to Muyenga and it was

strange to know that she would not be there. I remember her waking up on the day I left, just two weeks before. It was 4am and she woke to say goodbye to me. I told her that I would be back in two months. There was so much we still had to talk about and do.

The house was full of people paying their respects. The chairs had been moved to one side, the carpets rolled up and put away. There was a sense of sadness in the house but there was also a sense of order. She would have liked that. Compared to my father's funeral, it was now my generation making most of the decisions. We had come of age. We were getting guidance from the few elders who remained, stepping into those big shoes as we took on the mantle of eldership.

Since it was the Easter weekend, we chose to bury her on the Tuesday after Easter Monday. We sat up until late on Easter Sunday, typing up the order of service, choosing hymns, scripture readings and planning the next day. Estella and my nieces Elsa and Michelle chose the clothes and necklace she was to be buried in. Elsa and Michelle insisted on a necklace, as Maama loved beautiful things. Our friends Viola and Christine took it upon themselves to make sure we were eating and sleeping.

We woke up early the next morning and went to the funeral services to choose her coffin and give them the order of service. We left my cousin, Rev. Diana, another goddaughter of Maama's, there to finish off the arrangements while we went to the mortuary to see her and prepare her body. I wanted to help dress her as a way of paying my final tribute, until I saw her lying there, motionless, on a steel bed in the mortuary.

I touched her and she was cold. I wept when I told her how I had called and tried to speak to her and she would not take my call. How, when I finally got through, she was in too much pain to speak. I could not bear the thought of dressing her. So I sat outside and waited while Estella, Christine, Viola and my nieces dressed her. Then the funeral services people arrived with the hearse and coffin to take her to Muyenga, for her last night in her home.

At the time, my father's youngest brother, my godfather, Uncle Dennis, was bedridden with the last stages of cancer. He had not been able to come to our home for the wake, nor would he be at the funeral. He had been close to my mother and father. We felt unable to bury Maama without going to grieve with him and asking him if there was anything he wanted us to say at the funeral, so en route home we wanted to pass by his house and speak to him.

This presented us with a dilemma. We could not let the hearse go home without us; we had to be there to welcome Maama. However, we could not take the hearse all the way to Uncle's house, as people might think that he had died. Eventually we decided that when we got to Nakulabye, the suburb where Uncle Dennis lived, they should park the hearse nearby and wait for us while we went to speak to Uncle.

We drove from Mulago Hospital, a place my mother knew so well. I was born there, and she had nursed many people in that hospital: Fay and Chris, Maliza, Daddy, cousin Joyce, among others. We drove through Wandegeya, past Makerere University, her alma mater, and on to Nakulabye. We left her in the hearse by the roadside next to a nursery school, and went in to Uncle's house.

Uncle was lying in a hospital bed in his room, thin, his eyes large in his face. He managed a weak smile. We told him that

Maama had passed on and that her funeral was the next day. We told him we could not bury her without seeing and speaking to him. Then we prayed and sang together. As we were leaving, he said, 'Philippa, come here. I am your godfather. Tell me the truth: who is dead?' He simply could not believe she was gone. I told him again it was Maama, and tears rolled down his face. We spoke for a while and then I gave him a hug – the last hug we shared – and we left.

We drove Maama past the Kampala School for the Physically Handicapped, which she and my father had founded. We passed the Palace of the Kabaka, eSaawa ya Queen, through Nsambya to Kabalagala, past the market and John Rich Supermarket where she had shopped, past the Italian shop. Finally we were home.

Her body was wheeled into the sitting room. Rev. Diana, her husband Rev. Solomon, and other priests from All Saints Cathedral, where Maama had been a congregant since the 1960s, led us in prayers.

Two weeks after we buried Maama, Uncle Dennis passed away.

7 Rekindled

What makes a fire burn
is space between the logs,
a breathing space.
JUDY BROWN

When my father died, most of our children – my sisters' and cousins' children – were at the wake and the funeral. They noticed that we, our generation, all knew each other well – our cousins and our cousins' cousins. It was the same with our parents' generation. It was not the same for them, so they started what they called the 4th Generation.

At least once a term, during the school holidays in Kampala, they organised their own functions, asking for help only with money for food and transport. Their intention was to get to know each other. A few of the younger ones of my generation were also integrated into the 4th Generation. They became bridges, like Uncle Dennis was towards the end of his life, between his generation and ours. They encouraged people to bring their cousins, and partners if they were dating. They started a Facebook group and a Mxit group. When cousins came from outside Uganda, like my children did, they made sure there was a 4th Gene' get-together. They even had photo shoots.

Gatherings were often held at Maama's house because she would prepare her famous 'fish fingers' – tilapia marinated in her special way and gently fried – and would make sure they had more than enough to eat and drink, even when they said they would bring their own food. She loved having them around. In January 2009 they had a 4th Gene gathering when I was at home with Faye and Senteza, pregnant with Chris. I was in the sitting room with Maama, my sister Estella and a few others.

The 4th Generation were outside in the garden, their chairs in a circle. They had a ritual when beginning their gatherings because there was always someone new to the group. They each introduced themselves, and their cousins asked particular questions – about life, school, partners. Then they played games. As their laughter floated into the sitting room, we went onto the veranda to watch. It took me back to my own childhood.

I felt hopeful. Here they were, the next generation, forging links. I knew they had each other's backs. Even though the gatherings are not regular because they were all growing up, starting their own lives in different places – Uganda, South Africa, Kenya, the States, New Zealand – the fire had been lit and they knew who they were.

Echoes of a journey

2004

Dry and parched
restless
like the salt-filled breezes
of this land
I leave the mountain,
draped in its cloth,
early in the morning
and journey northward
bound for where
the Equator wraps itself
round the waist of my first home.

I arrive
in the land of the great Lake Nalubaale,
to the buzz of mosquitoes and lake flies
and the warm, humid
sky of dusk's purply embrace.
I am home.

I know I shall
wake up in a land
covered in green banana plantations,
mango trees and jack fruit,
reservoir of the stories and songs of my youth.
Maybe this land

will quench my thirst –

I rise to the smell of rain
on the red soil of family,
Daddy eating pawpaw with relish
Maama drinking another cup of tea
Estella hurrying slowly to get to town
and the children – Elsa, Michelle, Faye and Sente
screaming with laughter in the garden.
I drink from this love
potent in each life.

I drink too
of the embraced unspoken,
unasked, un-understood –
Maliza silent in her room
Fay and Chris, their smiles now only
pictures on the wall
beautiful lives held captive
in twisted urns
my heart aches with love expressed
and unexpressed.

Screaming to be released
the unspoken festers,
holding us hostage,
refusing to
let us go even as we
have never let it go.

The waters in the pot
of this first home
are bittersweet –

the thirst remains.

Twelve hours later
I journey east
to my second home
land of the Rift Valley,
mounts Kenya and Kilimanjaro.
Flying high, through blue
skies, expectant
I go to celebrate coming of age
with sisters turning 40.
It has been a long time.

We meet in this land
that too thirsts for water
savannah grasslands, thorn trees
brown hills, undulating –
I come here to drink
from the gourd of friendship,
will this thirst be quenched?

Kamiti – farms rich in coffee trees,
tea with Maama Njoki.
Boma – dorms rising over Five Acres,
squeals of delight and surprise – teenagers once again.
Athi River – laughter, tears,

silence
as we reminisce and celebrate,
share the gifts of lives lived.
Karen, Buru-buru, Hurlingham.
Visiting the places of my youth;
have I drunk enough?

I leave once again
my soul soaked
in home waters
marinated with
myriads of spokens and unspokens
seen and unseen,
embraced and unembraced.

I return south
to the home
by the mountain and the sea
quenched
rooted deeper
in red soil, savannah lands
and sand.

Travelling the 40-odd kilometres from Kampala to Entebbe
at 4am as my children and I left Uganda in January 2009, I
considered the significance of this road to me. It had symbol-
ised uncountable comings and goings, goodbyes and reunions,
happy days, sad days, joy and fear. Travelling this road, I had
seen the country change. I had changed, too, and so had the
road, and yet in some ways it was still the same. This was the

road that led to the Botanical Gardens, the zoo, Lake Victoria, the old and new airports, Nsamizi and State House Entebbe.

One of my earliest memories is going to the Botanical Gardens in Entebbe and then to the zoo. It was New Year's Day in 1972. We went with the whole family: Maama, Dad, Maliza, Estella, Fay, Chris and I; Aunty Ida, Joyce, Uncle Dennis; and 'the Uncle Hugos': Uncle, Aunty, Alice, Mire, Sema, Eddie and Zaw. My friend Patricia was with us. We ate sandwiches, rice and stew, roast chicken and cakes. Then we played games – all of us, the adults and the children together in teams. We loved running races. I loved the wheelbarrow race, the egg-and-spoon race, the sack race and the three-legged race. For the three-legged race I was coupled with Estella. We hobbled along and fell, then tried to get up again, laughing hysterically, trying so hard to win. Later we went to the zoo. The main attraction for me was a huge chimpanzee called Harry. We stood in front of his cage waiting, and then he rubbed his tummy, pointed to his head and made faces. We thought he was hilarious.

Then I remember Nsamizi, a hill in Entebbe where the Nsamizi Institute stood at its summit in the 1950s and 1960s. Jajja John had worked there as a teacher and he and Jajja Maliza lived in one of the staff houses. I remember one family gathering we had, around Christmas time. We had spent Christmas Day at Kabanyolo Farm with Uncle Hugo's family. Maama said I could stay for a few a nights and they would pick me up from Jajja's house when we all met there.

The day before we went to the Jajjas we made kites with paper, bamboo and string so that we could fly them out there. My cousins and I sat around the dining room table with a big craft book that had all the instructions. We were so excited that we were going to fly our kites the next morning. We travelled in Uncle Hugo's Saab, which had an extra backward-facing seat in the boot that took three passengers. We always fought to sit there. That day, Aunty Ntongo said it was my turn.

We met my parents and other family members at Nsamizi. There was good food, stories and laughter, and we flew our kites in the breeze from Lake Nalubaale (Lake Victoria), with the adults doing their best to help. At some point we sang, like we often did: children's play songs such as 'Nakyibosi wala nnyo, Nakyibosi wala', rounds like 'Row, row, row your boat', and 'Kookaburra sits in the old gum tree', remnants of our parents' missionary education. The African American spirituals, 'Oh freedom, oh freedom' and 'Kum ba yah' were also favourites. Then came the solos. I can still hear Aunty Jane, Daddy's youngest sister, playing her guitar and singing 'Hey Jude'. Her voice was soft and sultry.

In the early days, the trip to Entebbe was never about arriving. It was about what we saw and did on the way. From our house in Nakasero we would go past eSaawa ya Queen on Entebbe Road. We would each try to be the first one to see the statue of a bodybuilder outside the Turkish baths in Kajansi. Further along we often stopped on the roadside to see one old man's puppets and sculptures. His place seemed to appear just as we rounded one of the corners, and I was never sure when it would happen. We competed to see who would spot them first. We did not know who he was, why he made them, or if he sold them, but they were always part of the trip.

Then there was the house that was under construction for years and years, but never finished. People said it was haunted. In those days, traffic flowed easily and there were no roadblocks. We would pass by St Mary's Kisubi, a boys' school, and know that we still had a way to travel. Then, at a certain point, we would go down towards Lake Victoria and know we had arrived. That was the gateway into Entebbe.

Entebbe not only had the gardens, the zoo, the Lake Victoria Hotel and the beaches; it also had the airport, and travelling was a big thing. In the 1960s and 1970s we all dressed up smartly to go to the airport; there were no jeans and takkies. Often, carloads of relatives would travel to see someone off or welcome them home. After they had checked in, we would go upstairs to the deck so we could wave as they boarded the plane.

I was about eight or nine when Aunty Irene, my favourite aunt, was leaving for good. She was engaged to Uncle Mathias and they were leaving for Germany to get married. We'd had a grand party for them at our house at 1A Kafu Road, just before they left. Then the day came when we drove to the airport in three carloads. It was all okay until I saw them walk onto the runway towards the plane. Then it dawned on me that I might never see her again, and I cried inconsolably. She was the one who fetched us from school when my parents couldn't, and took us to the Wimpy and the drive-in. She baked the most delicious Easter biscuits and Christmas cakes. What would I do without her? I got everyone crying.

There were, and still are, markets on that road and often the trip back meant stopping to buy grapefruit, pawpaws, pineapples, matooke, bundizi and all sorts of vegetables. Daddy liked buying his grapefruit from a man called Mwami Greenson. The stop was not solely about the buying; it would be a moment for conversation about life, the family, the weather, the harvest. Once, a taxi driver who was passing by stopped us. My mother had taught him in primary school. He bought us fruit to take to her.

One day in the mid-1970s, when the new airport was opened and we went at night in our pyjamas to fetch Daddy on his return from a trip to Europe or Latin America, I simply stared as we approached the building: it looked like a million glowing candles.

As the years passed, the road to Entebbe slowly changed, and what was once an exciting ride became a stressful one. In the 1980s, all the anticipation and excitement of the previous years dissipated and a hollowness filled my stomach. The Obote II regime erected roadblocks, and at each one you were at the mercy of the soldiers manning the checkpoint.

The worst was just as you entered Entebbe. As you came down the hill, the lake appeared, reflecting the sky, drawing you closer. But a few metres on, there it was: the roadblock, busy and slow, guarded by soldiers 24 hours a day. They were unpredictable and acted with impunity, stopping you and sometimes searching through all your suitcases. Many people missed their flights, and some even had their money taken from them. As a result trips to Entebbe only happened when absolutely necessary. They were no longer for fun.

On this visit, I had arrived on Boxing Day 2008, accompanied by my children Faye and Sente. I carried within me the seed that was to be Christopher. It had taken us two hours to navigate the 40-odd kilometres to Kampala. The traffic was crazy. There were supposed to be two lanes on the road but there seemed to be five or six, with each impatient driver trying to get home quickly. The fear of the 1980s had gone, replaced by the mad rush of the twenty-first century: boda-bodas, the motorcycle taxis that operated by their own traffic rules; long traffic jams; and drivers who were no longer polite but drove to intimidate so they could pass. Peace had made way for another kind of madness.

And here I was again, for what felt like the millionth time, leaving home on this road.

Cape Town, too, becomes more like home every year. The homecoming, though, is different from the one in Uganda. Landing in Entebbe conveys a visceral knowing that I am home. From the moment the plane flies over Lake Nalubale, every part of my being wakes up. I am aware of the paradox of belonging – the love and irritation, joy and pain, the knowing and not knowing, that fact that even as I have left I am inextricably tied to this place. I sense the lightness and tensions in the air.

My ears prick-up to the soundscape: the crow of the cock and birdsong in the mornings, the buzz of mosquitos at night, the traffic, the familiar intonations of the different local languages and their flavouring of the English language, and the rumble of thunder distant or close. I can smell the rain coming.

My mouth moistens as taste buds remember beans cooked with omuzigo'muganda, kabalagala, kimisyebeebe, maleya cooked in a thick peanut sauce, spicy tea brewed in a pot with entangawuzi, tea masala or omudalasini, mangoes, sugar cane. My soles touch the ground and I feel the connections to generations of belonging.

Coming home to Cape Town has been a work in progress. At first it did not feel like coming home, because although there was relative peace, I was an outsider. I readied myself for the questions from people of all races. The white people asked, 'Where do you come from?'

'Uganda.'

'Oh, Idi Amin? Did you ever meet him?'

'No.'

'Why are you here?'

'I am a good wife,' I would reply with a smile.

'Oh, is your husband South African?'

'No, he is also Ugandan.'

'When are you going back?'

This question made me want to ask, 'Back to where?' This is my continent. I am at home.

Then came, 'Oh, you speak so well, did you study in the UK?'

'No. I was born and bred in Africa.' In those moments I was glad my surname was Kabali-Kagwa, and not my birth name, Barlow.

Then there were my black brothers and sisters who would get upset that I did not speak a local language. Some thought I was too proud.

In Maseru, an old Mosotho man said to me, 'You don't speak Sesotho because your parents sent you abroad?' When I told him that I spoke Luganda, he said, 'But you live here in Lesotho, you should speak Sesotho.' Sometimes I would reply to their questions in Luganda and keep speaking until they realised we did not speak the same language. At other times I tried to explain myself.

Uyathetha? Bua? Khuluma? Hayibo!

Cape Town 2006

'Molo Ma,' he says.
'Molo bhuti,' I reply. 'Full tank, 95.'
He opens the petrol tank, puts in the thingy and
fires a question to which I respond,
'Andisithethi isiXhosa. Ndiyathetha kancinci.'[8]
'Hau,' he says. 'Uyabua? ... Khuluma? ... Shangaan? ...
    Afrikaans?'
I shake my head with a half smile.
Here we go again, playing this game of
Who are you? Where do you fit?
I am transported to another place and time –

    Addis Ababa, 1979.
    A father and daughter drive up to a bakery
    outside a long line of people
    waiting for bread.

    They get out of the car
    walk past the line
    straight to the till
    and ask for bread.
    The people in the line murmur.

---

8. I don't speak Xhosa. I speak only a little.

The lady at the counter speaks to them abruptly in
  Amharic.
The father takes out his red ID book.
Foreigners, it says.
The murmurs grow louder.
They get their bread and walk away
looking no one in the eye.

'Sisi, are you Nigerian?'
I am rudely awakened from my reverie.
Nigerian?

'No, I come from Uganda.'
'Where?'
'Uganda.'
To my relief
he makes no quick references to Idi Amin
or HIV and AIDS,
only a blank stare.

His blank stare takes me back to another place in time.

  Oshakati, 1990.
  A young woman stands in line
  applying for a driver's licence.
  He insists on filling in the forms:
  'Where were you born?'
  'Kampala, Uganda.'
  He looks puzzled.
  She spells it, and he writes it all down.

She reads it upside down
'Place of Birth – Town: Kampala; District: Uganda;
        Country: Namibia.'
'Excuse me,' she says,
'Kampala is both the city and the district,
Uganda is the country.
It is not part of Namibia.'
He looks at her, puzzled.
'Angola?'
'No,' she says. 'Uganda. Near Tanzania.'
He puts his pen down and shakes his head.
'Difficult case,' he says.
'Go to Ondangwa.'
And moves on to the next person.

'Bhuti, I come from Uganda.
It is near Tanzania and DRC,' I say.
'Okay,' he replies, shrugging his shoulders.
'R300, Mama.'
I hand him the money, and drive off.

I arrived in Cape Town on the 1st of May 1993. Victor had come on the 31st of December 1992. He returned to Oshakati at the end of April to fetch Faye and me. We drove from Oshakati, about 2000 kilometres, to Tygerberg Hospital, where Victor was starting his training. South Africa was in flux. Chris Hani had just been killed and we had no idea what would happen. Would there be peace, or would there be war? We were not sure whether it would have been better for me to keep a base in Namibia, just in case, until things settled. However, we also wanted to be together, to raise our daughter together. We had been in Lesotho when Mandela was released and we had hope.

Looking back, I realise that we were naive about the complexities of South African society. We had never lived in a place where our blackness determined where we stayed, where we studied, how we travelled, where we shopped. We understood apartheid in our heads, but we had no experience of it. This was probably both a blessing and a curse. If we had known then what we know now, we would have been extremely nervous about coming to stay at Tygerberg, a decidedly Afrikaans institution. Our lack of a lived experience of apartheid enabled us to step into places we otherwise might not have gone, and to ask questions we otherwise might not have asked.

I remember one evening a young white Afrikaans doctor and his wife invited us out for dinner. We drove with them to Voortrekker Road in Parow, up the road from Tygerberg, and walked into a popular restaurant. It was noisy as we approached the door, and when we walked in it changed to a loud quiet. Everyone turned and stared at us. We were shocked but decided we weren't leaving. We sat down and soon people started talking again. Our hosts apologised. I think they too were shocked. We all tried to ignore what had happened, making small talk, eating, but well aware that people were watching us.

Tygerberg was built with two wings that were mirror images of each other. The west wing was for white patients and the east wing for black patients. The west side of the hospital property also had a nurses' hostel for white nurses and a doctors' quarters for white doctors. The east side had a nurses' hostel for black nurses but no doctors' quarters. Black doctors had never been in the plan.

On the 1st of February 1993, the doctors, nurses, students and porters all worked together to integrate the wards in the hospital, moving some of the white patients to the east wing, and some the black patients to the west wing. When Victor told me about it on the phone, before we joined him, I had struggled to understand, but then it started to make sense.

We were the first black African family to live in the doctors' quarters. There was also an Indian family. The doctors' quarters had five floors made up of mainly one-bedroomed apartments. At the end of each floor there was a two-bedroomed apartment. We lived in B51. Below us, in B41, was a Polish family with three children – two boys and a little girl. In B31 was the Indian family from Durban, with two children – a boy and another girl. In B21 was another Polish family with a son. B11 housed a white South African family, from out of town, with son. Each family had a child about Faye's age.

Our children brought us together, all except the family in B21, who tended to keep to themselves. Whenever one of the children saw the others outside they would want to go and play. The mothers followed the children and soon we started talking to each other. None of us had friends or extended family in Cape Town so we became a support system for each other. Our lives revolved around the children and keeping house. Our husbands were all studying and working. Each one of us longed for some free time.

After a month or so of our children playing together, we started inviting each other home for a coffee and soon set up a playgroup. Every Tuesday morning two of us would look after all the kids, while the other two slept in, did housework, went shopping, or went to watch the cheap Tuesday morning movie at the Sanlam Centre in Parow. Or if we had time, we'd make a quick trip to the factory shops at Access Park in Kenilworth. It was lovely.

We also took a few trips to Blouberg beach during the summer. Heidi, the white South African, had a kombi that we all piled into. It must have been a strange experience for the other beachgoers. It was the first time for all those women to have a black friend. I was surprised. I remember Ayesha, the Indian lady, speaking to me about it and telling me about growing up in Natal, before it merged with KwaZulu. She gave me a necklace before she left, and I still wear it.

As Victor and I started to understand South African society, our biggest challenge became how to build a home for our children that gave them a sense of belonging. We were concerned about giving them strong black role models like we'd had, so we began to create an extended family of special friends from all over. We also tried to go back to Uganda every two years so our children would get to know home.

In December 1998 my sister Estella was getting married. I was to be the matron of honour and my children were in the bridal party. Victor could not come because he had just finished his master's and was starting to set up his practice.

About a month before the trip I went to Home Affairs to renew our work permits. This was an annual practice for us, and I applied for our work permits and the children's visas. I was told to come back in two weeks to collect them. When I went back they weren't ready. The day before we left they were still not ready, but the lady at the counter said we could go to Uganda with the receipts and they would forward my work permit and the visas to the High Commission in Uganda. So we left.

The wedding was great fun. It was the first time my children had been to one because we didn't belong enough yet in South Africa to be invited to weddings. After Christmas I went to the High Commission to follow up on our documents. They were not there. I phoned Victor and my office at the Teacher Inservice Project, and went to the High Commission regularly. It took us about six weeks to get the visas and get back to Cape Town. The children were late for school and I missed many days of work. How could I call Cape Town home?

The good thing to come out of the delay, though, was that we spent longer at home than we had planned. Faye and Senteza, then seven and two-and-a-half years old, bonded with their cousins, all their grandparents and my aunts and uncles, and I loved being part of the community rituals that I missed in South Africa.

One of my first jobs in Cape Town was working for the Teacher Inservice Project at the University of the Western Cape. We worked with schools, mostly in the black and coloured townships, with the staff and governing bodies, facilitating change and development processes. It was a time of policy change, so we also mediated policy for the schools, helping them implement it in their particular school, and match it with their vision and mission.

Often we worked with schools for a couple of years and got to know the staff well. I worked in Khayelitsha, Lwandle and Nomzamo, Somerset West and Mbekweni, and in farm schools in Wellington and Paarl. It was a great education for me. In some of the schools I developed real trust with teachers, and they would challenge me when I made incorrect assumptions. I could challenge them too.

I learnt how to get around the townships and realised that, for the most part, it was okay. It was not as frightening as the people in the doctors' quarters made it out to be. Real people lived and worked there. I learnt how to read the context, to know if everything was okay, like I had in Kampala.

The farm schools I worked at sometimes had three or four grades in one little church building, some with only two or three teachers. I was impressed by their dedication. One school had no water, and each child had to bring their own water in a two-litre bottle.

There were many times when I was part of a workshop that was mostly in Afrikaans, or where the issues were more easily discussed in isiXhosa. Having been an outsider for most of my life, I had learnt that language is not a barrier. People use the language they understand best to discuss things, especially things close to their hearts.

I drew on my experience from when I taught in Ongwediva, Namibia, where I had students with varying levels of fluency in English. Sometimes I would look at them and know that only a handful understood what I was saying. I started identifying those who were fluent in English, and when I thought it was necessary, I would stop, and ask them to explain to their classmates in Oshiwambo. I watched, and when I saw people nodding, and heard enough 'Mmm's and 'Eh's, I spoke again, asking questions to check understanding. So in Cape Town I did the same. I would ask someone to translate, listen deeply, read body language, and check to make sure we were on the same page. I learnt to ask questions without being afraid of looking stupid.

It took us about eight years to get permanent residence, and it was only then that I began to call Cape Town home. It is a big city, divided along race and class lines in blatant and subtle ways. Having lived in many multiracial communities, I found Cape Town to be one of the loneliest places I have lived. In spite of that, I have made some good friends over the years, and my children have become true Capetonians.

Then in January 2008, as my roots were deepening, we had an armed robbery at home.

It was the night before the school year began. I was watching TV with my sister-in-law, Marion, and my husband's aunt, Maama Dorcas. They were visiting us, along with my parents-in-law. My mother-in-law was in an adjacent room reading, and my father-in-law was downstairs getting a drink from the bar. My 16-year-old daughter was taking a shower, and my 12-year-old son was busy on his PlayStation in another room. We heard the garage door open as my husband returned home. It was about 8.30pm.

All of a sudden I heard my husband shout, a deep guttural sound, as if something was really wrong. There was scuffling downstairs. Maama Dorcas and I stood at the top of the stairs, peering down to see what had happened.

My first thought was that my father-in-law had collapsed. Then we saw my husband running up the stairs. He ran straight past us and out onto the balcony. He did not say a word. Two men, waving guns, were running behind him.

At first we had a sense of disbelief, and then I shouted, 'What did you do to them?' In my mind, people only chased you because they were angry. Then the cold realisation that we were being robbed set in.

Victor managed to get onto the balcony unseen, jumped

down two storeys, and climbed over the fence to the neighbours' house. They called the armed response. The men walked around nervously asking where he was. This is probably what saved us.

Faye was in the bathroom with her phone. She sent out a *Please Call Me* to our priest, Tony, and to her music teacher, but they did not respond. Then she remembered what her preschool teacher, Mrs Loggenberg, had drummed into their heads: 'If you are ever in trouble at home, call the police on 10111.' So she did that.

The robbers did not stay long, and the police never caught them. Victor came back just after the police arrived. I let him in and, in the confusion, the police chased us onto our balcony at gunpoint, thinking that he was one of the robbers and had taken me hostage. I found myself shouting, 'We all belong here. We all belong here. This is my husband!'

The incident awakened some of the latent fears and survival instincts we had learnt growing up in Uganda, but we were determined to be okay, even though Victor had dislocated his shoulder when he jumped, and had to spend the night in hospital. I got up the next morning, took the kids to school, spoke to their teachers about what had happened, and behaved as normally as I could. For the next few months though, every little noise made us jumpy. Our sense of home had been shaken.

Then in May we witnessed the advent of what became a nationwide spread of xenophobic attacks on African 'foreigners'. As it started, it took me back to my time in Namibia. When I had eventually got a job at Ongwediva College of Education, I was excited because I would be training teachers, which felt like a privilege to me. I was also excited because the college had a mix of staff from all over: local Namibian teachers, UN volunteers from Tanzania, Sierra Leone and Somalia, volunteers from Denmark, and teachers from Iran and the Philippines. A few months after I started working there, a group of young American Peace Corps volunteers joined the college and surrounding schools. It was like the United Nations.

During this time the regulations around appointments started to change with the changing curricula. Some of the staff members did not have university degrees, even though they had taught at the college for a while. The new regulations required all staff to have degrees, or to be in the process of getting them. This enraged them because some of them were forced to look for work teaching in schools.

The levels of unemployment were high and there were demonstrations in the town, particularly by educators and nursing staff saying that foreigners were taking their jobs. When you asked a few questions, the foreigners turned out to be all the other Africans. The Pilipinos, Americans, Danes and Finns were seen as experts coming in to impart knowledge, regardless of their background and experience.

This made me angry, especially when I discovered that all my African colleagues at the college were qualified teachers who each had close to 20 years of experience. I was the youngest, having been on the job for four years. On the other hand, some of the others had no qualifications as teachers or in teaching subjects, yet were holding senior positions in various departments. Nevertheless, they were the experts in the eyes of the public.

At a general meeting in Windhoek, I commented that one could not assume that someone was qualified just because they came from Europe or the States. I pointed out that some of the Peace Corps volunteers were very young and had little or no work experience. It did not go down well.

A week later I ran into Hanu, a friend and colleague who was also acting rector at the college. He asked me if I had seen the local newspaper. I hadn't. He said there was something there about me. I bought a copy and found a letter to the editor about the meeting, arguing that I was a foreigner taking a local's job, and saying that I did not want any experts to come and help Namibians. I was angry and upset. I felt that I had been misquoted, but I did not want to start an I-said-she-said con-versation in the newspapers either. I told Hanu I would not respond, but if he wanted to respond as rector, since he had been at the meeting, I would appreciate it.

Hanu addressed it in the staff meeting because he believed it was an inside job. Many of the issues raised came out of the meeting we'd had in Windhoek. Some of the staff were support-ive of me, and others chose to say nothing. I kept quiet. Hanu wrote a supportive response in the paper and the whole thing died a natural death. However, for me it highlighted the fact that, no matter how close I felt to people, at some point I would always be an outsider.

Now, in my new home, foreigners were being targeted. What had started as a localised incident in Alexandra Township in Gauteng had spread to Cape Town and other cities. People were leaving their homes looking for refuge. Our church, Bel-lville Presbyterian, which is predominantly white, was offered as a refuge, and a group SMS was sent out asking for whatever help we could offer.

My gut response to the situation when I heard was to put

all the clothes, shoes and blankets that we were not using into a bag and take them to the church. As I drove back home, I reflected on the different feelings rising in me: a deep sense of fear, of needing to protect myself, my children, my husband, and my friends, as well as a profound need to do something, to make a difference and not let the fear take hold. A need to dull the fear with love.

I wanted to speak out and say we were all brothers and sisters, children of Africa. I wanted to act and make a difference. And yet I held back from further action. I felt vulnerable, like I could become a victim too. I also felt that when I went to the church the 'refugees' looked at me suspiciously, because I could pass for a South African. In my head the questions – *Who are you? Where do you belong? Why are you here?* – came rushing back. I felt the fear rising within me, a fear that almost paralysed me, taking me back to other moments in my life.

Then someone organised a concert at the Baxter Theatre, to raise money to support those who were displaced. A few months before, Cape Town musician Neo Muyanga had put together 'the Kwaya' – a multicultural, multigenerational vocal group that practiced every Saturday morning at the Unitarian church. It had become home for me. We played with our voices – singing songs, creating harmonies, or learning some of Neo's arrangements. When he suggested that we sing at that concert, we agreed. I felt that this was a place where I could contribute with passion.

Now, when I return to Cape Town I look out and see the mountain. I no longer feel my innards steel themselves against the loneliness, the questions, the voice that says 'you are not from here'. It has been 23 years since we arrived, and each year I peel away a layer of otherness and embrace a deeper sense of home-coming. I know bits of some local languages – enough to greet and make a little small talk. I have friends and an extended family, both real and created. My children belong here. They belong in Uganda too. I now feel a sense of coming to a home that I am building, weaving threads of my past with threads of my present, and creating a place of belonging.

Glossary

Acholi: Ugandan people who live in the northern part of Uganda, further north than the Langi.

akatogo ka muwogo n'ebijanjalo: a one-pot meal consisting of a bean stew and cassava. *See also 'katogo'.*

amawulire: the news.

anti: this word has many meanings depending on the context. Here it means 'you know'.

bakisimba: this word has two meanings. It is both the big drum that plays the main rhythm of the Kiganda dance, and one of the dances. Here it refers to the dance.

Bamasaba: Ugandan people who live in the eastern part of the country, on the slopes of Mount Elgon, or Mount Masaba, as they call it. They are sometimes referred to as the Bagisu. These are my mother's people.

bamjiddad: an Anglicisation of the Luganda phrase meaning 'you have been visited'.

bannange: this word has many different meanings depending on context. Here it means 'Oh my goodness.'

bogoya: big, sweet yellow bananas.

bundizi: small, sweet yellow bananas.

Damali nkusigudde: a Luganda phrase used to capture the rhythm of the drums.

dengu: green lentils.

doodo: a type of spinach.

ebugga: a type of spinach.

ekyinyebwa: a thick groundnut sauce.

empombo: stews and sauces steamed in soft banana leaves.

eSaawa ya Queen: Queen's Clock Tower on Entebbe Road, built to commemorate the visit of Queen Elizabeth II to Uganda from the 28th to the 30th of April 1954.

gonja: sweet, yellow plantains that are either steamed in their skins, grilled over a fire or sliced and deep fried.

jajja: grandmother or grandfather. A unisex term. The anglicised plural, jajjas, refers to grandparents.

kabaka: king.

kabaka anjagala: literally, 'the king [of Buganda] loves me.' Kabaka anjagala trees are candlenut trees, which line the avenue to the Buganda parliament.

kabalagala: a deep-fried pancake made from sweet bananas and cassava flour. Traditionally it would have a touch of chilli pepper to give it some zing.

katogo: a one-pot meal usually consisting of plantains or cassava as the starch; and meat, beans or a thick groundnut stew. *See also* 'akatogo ka muwogo n'ebijanjalo'.

Khukhu: grandmother, in Lumasaaba.

khuluma: talk, in isiZulu.

kimisyebeebe: pumpkin leaves, a delicacy among Bamasaaba.

kondo: thief.

kuwondowa: freewheel down the hill.

Lake Nalubaale: the Baganda call Lake Victoria 'Lake Nalubaale'.

Langi: Ugandan people from the central-northern part of Uganda, north of Lake Kyoga.

Lingala: a language spoken in Zaire (now the Democratic Republic of Congo). In those days a lot of the music we listened to was from Zaire – bands such as Tabu Ley Rochereau and Orchestra Super Mazembe.

Luhya: Kenyan people from the western side of Kenya, close to Uganda, who speak a language similar to Lumasaba, the language of my mother's people.

lusuku: banana garden.

maayi: mother in Lumasaaba.

matooke: green plantains that are peeled, wrapped in banana leaves and steamed, or cooked as a one-pot meal with beans or groundnut sauce. This is the staple food of many tribes in Uganda.

mbu: allegedly.

Mount Masaba: the Bamasaba call Mount Elgon, Mount Masaba.

mukeeka: a mat woven out of reeds or grasses, commonly used in Ganda households.

muwafu: *Canarium schweinfurthii*; the incense tree.

muwogo: cassava.

Naguru: a prison that was infamous during Amin's time. It was one of a few places that people knew the intelligence men took prisoners and tortured them.

nakati: greens related to the tomato family.

nti: that.

omudalasini: cinnamon.

omuzigo'muganda: ghee.

panga: machete.

Shangaan: A language spoken in the northern part of South Africa.

UVS: it was believed that the secret state security operatives, all drove cars whose number plates started with UVS or UVR.

uyabua: do you speak?

wama tugende: come on, let's go.

weeraba: goodbye.

Acknowledgements

There are many people I would like to thank for the birthing of this book, and many will be left out because of space.

To my parents, my first storytellers, who taught me about the power of story and books. My siblings – Maliza, Estella, Fay and Chris, and my borrowed ones – I love you all.

My sister–friend Getrude Matshe, who encouraged me to write the book in 2013, and to publish, thank you – your passion, insight and encouragement have been invaluable. Dorian 'Storian' Haarhoff, for your support as a writing mentor over the years. Godfrey Mukasa, Viola Mukasa, Dan Mudido and Alice Barlow-Zambodla for the translations from Luganda into English. Maria Serrano for your invaluable advice on translation. Giles Griffin for your meticulous proofreading and support when we called the book SOTAF – thank you.

My sisters and cousins, the 3rd Generation – I wouldn't swop you for anyone else. David Kitongo, thank you for connecting me with Catherine from Sardinia Restaurant. Maggie Bisase, thank you for sharing your memories and asking Aunty Flora. Moses Kinobe, thank you for being the family archivist.

I am eternally grateful for my sister-circle: Deirdre Prins-Solani, for slowly nudging, for reading and giving feedback, for reminding me about self-care; Malika Ndlovu for inspiration, support and the feedback you gave me; Yvonne Owuor for reading an early draft and spurring me on – meeting you in Addis was ordained; Mshai Mwangola for the Artists as Peacebuilders course and all that you are; Nyana Kakoma – you weren't the first to tell me to send my manuscript to Modjaji, but something struck home when you did. Birgitte Davy, Mandy Barnes, Maggi Baliddawa, Wacango Kimani, Irene Mureithi, Janet Awimbo, Veronica Mukasa, Irene Mukiri and Wamuni Njoroge for your constant friendship, and for making me part of your families. Madalina Florea for your encouragement.

My book club, the 13 African Moons, for the writers' retreat we had, and for sharing books with me. To the Woman Zone team – for publishing the first part of my story, for creating a space for women to share their stories, and for believing. Special thanks to Nancy Richards. To my storyteller friends, especially Sue Hollingsworth, Gilly Southwood and Gcina Mhlope for reminding me every day of the power of stories.

To Andie Miller for the prodding, asking, listening, shaping and keeping on going, even when we both wanted to throw our toys out – thank you. And to Colleen Higgs for starting Modjaji, and for agreeing to publish my book.

To Juliet Chinokopota and Monica Njomba for supporting me in the home so that I could juggle writing, working and motherhood – thank you.

And lastly to my family in Cape Town – Victor, Faye, Sente and Chris – thank you for enduring all my late nights and cranky days and for supporting me. I love you all.

About the author

Philippa Namutebi Kabali-Kagwa is a storyteller, leadership coach and facilitator. Starting out as a teacher, her work has grown into the areas of leadership and personal development. Philippa spoke at TEDxTableMountain and TEDxPrinceAlbert in 2012. She has published poems in a number of collections and has written four children's books.

Printed in the United States
By Bookmasters